Is This Really My Life?

Life is a Trip With or Without Hallucinogenics
Discover Meaning and Purpose as You Take the Ride

Sarah Wilcox

Founder, Women Included Now

Is This Really My Life?

ISBN: 978-1-7355709-0-7

Book design by: Christopher Derrick for Unauthorized Media.

Printed, in the United States of America.

First printing edition 2020.

While the author has made every effort to provide accurate internet addresses at the time of publication, the author assumes no responsibility for errors or changes that occur after publication.

WOMEN
INCLUDED NOW

DEDICATION

*To all the women who feel stuck and can't comprehend how they
will ever do it all without losing their minds and their souls.
To Craig, Anna and Matthew for your unending love and support.
To Sonia, for giving me the confidence
to show the world what I have to offer.*

Contents

INTRODUCTION

THIS BOOK IS FOR WOMEN WHO WANT TO BE THEIR best without sacrificing who they really are and what's important to them. It's the perennial question of how to get what you want without losing yourself along the way. As a woman, corporate executive, entrepreneur, wife, and mother, I found myself asking this question over and over as I managed life's responsibilities while trying not to lose track of my own identity.

I've written this book as a guide to help women, like yourself, discover who you are, where your joy comes from, and how acknowledging gratitude is one of the best tools in your arsenal for finding truth and meaning. I can't answer for you what gifts and talents you've brought into this life, but I'll show you how I identified what mine are and what I did with them. Throughout the following chapters, I'll share with you the way I went about developing my personal roadmap to put self, career, family, and community together in a way that made sense to me and brought about the most joy and satisfaction. You'll see that it hasn't been a straight line or always pretty, but I have to admit I like where I've ended up. I've also come to understand that roadmaps are living documents that don't end until the very end. They represent our evolution as individuals moving from one juncture to another, always seeking truth as we crystalize what brings us the most meaning and purpose.

Although my life is unique, as is yours, I've approached life as a puzzle to solve and have gone about trying to turn over as many stones as possible along the way – ensuring that I live a well-investigated life. I'm an experience junky and have always enjoyed changing my spots, which has meant that I've had lots of growth opportunities to explore what drives me. These experiences have shaped me and, ultimately, showed me how not to be afraid of taking risks even when the outcome is unknown.

We're all searching for something. It's the most time consuming, human pastime that I can think of and the basis for great expressions of creativity, innovation, and purposeful living. More often than not, while sitting on this planet making mayhem, we're looking to find the true essence of who we are as individuals and what we really desire from our lives. For most of us, it's the most important thing we will do during our 80-odd years of living and one that takes dogged determination.

Is This Really My Life? is a book of essays around ideas that I've contemplated and found beneficial in discovering who I wanted to be, and how I needed to go about putting the pieces together in a way that is a true expression of who I am. This quest always fascinated me because I knew that I was here on Earth to do more than work and buy things. Actually, I needed it to be about more than purchasing habits. I can't imagine agreeing to fly a million miles a year for my job just to own a luxury car. The question of one's life purpose is harder to nail down. I've come to understand that for me, meaning and purpose come from my relationships, adventures, and love of learning. Discovering what brings meaning and purpose to your life is like matching a key with the right keyhole. It's the best way I know to create a fulfilling life with no regrets.

Besides finding meaning in my life through a career and educational pursuits as well as parenting and partnering, purpose in life for me has meant that I will never be reconciled to the idea that my life is solely transactional and me-centered. We're all here to contribute something to society, both big and small. Although I'm not done answering all of my questions about human existence, it's been worth the sorting and consideration that I've spent on it so far. At this point, I've concluded that all of us won't be truly satisfied unless we're feeding both our souls and our bellies.

After years of working in corporate offices, I made the decision early this year to spend my time and energy helping other women bring it on. Although times have changed for women since I started ferreting out a career, it hasn't changed enough to allow many of us to make our greatest contributions to the world. Many of us still work two jobs, including at home and the office, struggle to be seen and heard, and often feel isolated in cultures that operate from a place of masculine power only. Team diversity and female leadership are still in paltry quantities in most companies, even though research has shown that the most productive teams of people use diverse experiences and perspectives to manifest innovation. As women with greater opportunities than any other generations before us, we have the chance to put our hearts and minds together and explore what we want as individuals as well as what gifts and talents we can provide to the broader community.

Introspection comes naturally to some people and, consequently, the inner world of one's being is available for gathering insights and finding meaning in life. For others, we're experiential learners and find our truth via trial and error. And for a good many of us, it's a trek through the outer and inner walls of our lives conjoined that teach us what we need to know to thrive. The primary requirement to living a life of meaning and purpose is that you have to be willing to learn. You also have to be willing to put into action what you know to be true.

For years, many of us have tried to separate our work and personal lives. In fact, companies tried to mandate that we keep them apart for fear our sniveling children and chaotic home lives would distract us from being productive employees focused on the business at hand. But as the years have evolved, and our collective desires have changed, we've found that creating an integrated life is more in keeping with living an authentic life. It's impossible to cut ourselves off from our deepest desires and concerns for eight hours a day or longer. And we're no longer willing to do it.

Giving yourself space and time to search for what you truly want out of life is fundamental to finding answers to questions of meaning and purpose. If you're as impatient as I have been, you want all the answers to come quickly and without pain. For years, I saw life as black and white binary choices and hoped that it would unfold in a flawless canopy of splendor. I'm pretty sure by now you've had to move on, as I have, to the realization that life is offering us a winding journey, one that hopefully we'll be on for decades. There will be bumps along the way, and we'll become bruised at times, but be assured we'll also find happiness, love, and success on our terms.

As you read through the following essays about how I approached my search for meaning and purpose in life as well as how I learned to embrace my true identity, I hope you find the ideas worth exploring in your own life. We're really not all that different from one another, rather, the same china set only with chips and decals that are all our own. I wish you hope, presence of mind, and loads of laughter along the way.

Section I

Looking For You

Often, we find "ourselves" transitioning from moments of exhilaration to despair, swinging high, then low, and back to feeling good again. Some of these experiences occurred because of choices we made or actions we took while others seem to have come out of the ether. Sifting through our life's journey thus far shows us what we dropped along the way, what we need to pick up, and who we truly desire to become.

....

ONE

UNPLANNED MOUNTAINS

Today, I can safely say that I've survived, succeeded somewhat, and failed innumerable times to achieve goals I set in my 20's. Life over these past few decades has been a blur of corporate burn out, entrepreneurial quicksand, marriage partnering, and mommyhood. It's all brought me to the conclusion that every life is filled with unexpected surprises, shocking moments of dread and terror, and periods of ecstasy. It's a trip with or without hallucinogenics.

"Is this really my life?" is a perfectly reasonable question to ask yourself, especially after a reporter called you an overpaid flack in his newspaper column for an entire year because he hated your boss. Or after your three-year-old son woke you from a dead sleep with a kickbox to your bedroom door for 14 days in a row. Or was it 14 months? It's even the right question to ask when you can't figure out what the heck you were supposed to be when you grew up. Scientist? No, that wasn't it. Professional skier? Doubtful. Stay-at-home mom? Ooh, too hard. What did I think my life was really going to look like? I, certainly, couldn't have predicted it would consist of one unplanned mountain to climb after another. I thought it was more of a sure thing.

Most of us are terrified at the idea that life will throw us unplanned mountains that we can't handle. We try to avoid them, but ultimately, they're well represented on our tour of duty called life. What trips us up most of the time is our emotional reaction to life not working out as planned. Whether an unplanned mountain is health-related, financial, or love, there are ways of pushing through to the other side. It's the tantrums, depression, and flat-out hysteria that gets in our way. Aging doesn't always correlate to maturity. Being told to "act like a grown-up" doesn't help either.

Adulting begins the moment you're unceremoniously launched out of a cannon into the world of independent living. Most of us have the same sudden impact experience – smiling parents waving good-bye to their newly minted adult child as you back out of the driveway and head for your first real job. I left home with dreams, hopes, and an unwavering idealism that life would work out. I returned home for Christmas as a realist living in a cockroach-infested apartment on the Upper Westside of New York, defiant in my belief that I was on my own. And was I ever.

I moved to New York because I wanted a job in journalism. I was well-armed with an English Lit. degree and some bad poetry I had written during a particularly painful breakup. I found a job as an executive assistant, which is a moniker for "secretary." I typed, ran errands, and hovered in the doorways of the editors drooling over their very important work. It was also the year our federal government closed all of the psychiatric hospitals so patients could use community mental health services, which never materialized. Needless to say, there was a very high concentration of mentally ill patients living in my rent-controlled neighborhood. All in all, my transition from small-town girl to big-city working stiff was a shock I've just recently recovered from.

On reflection, I see my New York experience as my first unplanned mountain that I had to climb. You have yours as well but may call it something different, such as "your mistake, failure, crossroad or liftoff to hell." It's when there's a disconnect between what you imagined your life would look like and what is actually happening in real life. You see, we don't envision life being an upward climb. For God's sake, we're Americans! We say things like, "moving up the corporate ladder," but what we really mean is that we'll have a seamless rise to more money, prestige, and choice of automobiles. We don't really mean we're up for an oxygen-gasping, white-knuckled steep climb on an impassable, sheer-cliff mountain. Whoa, that would be way too exhausting and terrifying. Right?

I use the unplanned mountain descriptor to describe those times when you've entered territory that is utterly foreign and thought to be completely unnecessary if you had any say in the matter. It works well with the British slang word, "gobsmacked," which means to be more than just surprised. It's used for something that leaves you speechless, or otherwise stops you dead in your tracks. Yes, that would be how I feel when I'm climbing that unplanned mountain.

Unplanned mountains are events and situations that would never find their way onto your personally designed map. They show up unexpectedly and create serious mood swings, including anxiety, and a whole lot of growth opportunities. They're inevitable in both our personal and professional lives. For example, did you see that merger coming on the horizon? The one that would eventually downsize most of the people from your side of the business. How about the diagnosis of ADD in your youngest child that would leave him running for the hills every time the morning school bell rang – literally, running out the door day-after-day, year-after-year. Definitely didn't see these as part of my plan.

It's hard not to compare your unplanned events with other people. It's not like a status thing where you claim, "My unplanned mountain is bigger than yours." It's more like, "Boy, my life sucks right now while yours looks pretty impressive from here." Unplanned mountains can wreak havoc on your self-esteem. I've often resorted to wine and ice cream as sedatives as I was doing many of my climbs. I just wish it made me feel better to overeat and become intoxicated as an added benefit to all the weight and bleariness that actually resulted. The truth is that the only way to manage an unplanned mountain is to face it head-on into the wind.

Unplanned mountains are clearly the defining moments of adulthood. We begin our adulting phase knowing that it isn't going to be anywhere near as much fun as elementary school recess. But let's face it, we're all completely unprepared for how our particular unplanned climbs will wind around the mountain face. We know they're in our future, we just don't know which ones we're going to have to handle.

Based on my parent's history, I was fully prepared for mental illness and addictions. I suspected a 12-step program would be in my future even before I took my first drink and had a list of therapists on speed dial. Turns out, I only needed the therapist, and that was because of the other people in my life and not me. Okay, maybe that's not really true. But the twists and turns I found myself maneuvering in my career were never part of my parents' experiences. They also had four children who not once got caught by the police doing something illegal. We also all managed to be out of the house by the time we were 21. Whereas, my husband and I had to escort our daughter to city court on a littering charge for overreacting when her girlfriend threw an open female condom at her, and she tossed it out the window. Luckily, the arresting officer didn't show, so the case was thrown out. And my son still lives with us and shows no sign of leaving.

When I reflect on my career and life experiences, I can decisively pick out those moments when I was "gobsmacked," and left open-mouthed gaping at the sheer misdirection I found myself driving toward. Even after all these years, I wonder if I could have read my cues better and planned my life with more precision, but as my family will attest, I have no sense of direction whatsoever. Walking out of an elevator and determining the correct direction to walk is a 50-50 proposition that I often fail at. My son has decided that my tombstone will read: "Where Am I?"

I decided to write about unplanned mountains because while it's fun to read about someone else's missteps, it can also be instructional to learn how someone else finished her climb. Instead of shaking your head in disbelief and sharing thoughts of, "I would never want Sarah's life" or, "How in the world did she get into that mess?" I'm hoping my unplanned mountain stories will move you to pour yourself another glass of wine and exclaim, "She's one lucky woman to still have all her marbles!" Because really, that's about all I've been able to retain over these many years.

The truth is no one is exempt from the reality of unplanned mountains to climb. At one time or another, we all find ourselves in an unplanned mountain that feels like a game of Escape Room. Our job is to devise the least painful strategy for extricating ourselves. Sometimes your reflexes are quick enough to dodge the hard-hitting objects, but other times you finish your unplanned climb bruised and mildly catatonic. In retrospect, you may find humor in what happened to you while you weren't looking. Sometimes you just need more therapy or ice cream to move forward.

Life's unplanned mountains are worth thinking about both before and after you've identified yours. For instance, throughout the years, I would make a mental note of the unplanned mountains I definitely never, ever wanted to experience. I managed to avoid a few, including when I declined a position with the Peace Corps because Idi Amin, aka the "Butcher of Uganda," was ransacking East Africa, and the volunteers were huddled in the U.S. Embassy hoping to live to see another day. I also managed to marry a man who was actually good for me and haven't needed the assistance of a divorce lawyer in almost 30 years. He's remained kind, funny, and smart, and over the years, has allowed me to drag him into many different escapades he would not have chosen for himself.

The truth is I could have taken more control of my career and bank account over the years and missed out on some of the more notable unplanned mountains I climbed. I just didn't know I had that kind of power over my life. While in college, my dad used to tell me to "cooperate and graduate," so obviously, my role model wasn't the designer of his own destiny either. Dad was a great guy, but not a poster boy for the much-used adage, "taking the bull by the horns." He was timid in how he approached life and, therefore, never fully engaged with other people and rarely went after the things he could have been passionate about. He went into law because his father and brother expected him to join the family law firm. I'm pretty sure he would have been much happier coaching a sports team at the local high school. Life events, however, play a big part in how much appetite we have for risk. When my father came back from World War II, he was incredibly grateful to be alive and back in the United States. He felt he had already won the lottery. Why tempt fate again?

I have a much higher tolerance for risk than my father had, but I grew up in a generation that actively pursued change. (It's true we dropped the ball a few years back and are now doing a handoff to the younger generations. Sorry about that.) We thought of ourselves as empowered and masters of our universe, which explains why I'm really drawn to the new label of "badass" women. I connect with the implication that women can handle whatever life throws our way. Being a "badass" means you have the confidence and perseverance to defy the downward spiral of an unplanned mountain and move on to creating life on your own terms. I even joined an online women's group because I liked their name, *League of Badass Women*. All of this brings me to my earlier point, which is that you need to be able to muster enough courage to become unstoppable when an unplanned mountain shows up.

I don't recommend the use of drugs or food for conquering un-planned mountains. You need all the clarity you can muster at these times. When you find yourself facing an unplanned mountain, it's best to remind yourself that it's just a moment in time in your long life. Uncomfortable situations are unavoidable, so when they occur, keep repeating to yourself, "Breathe. Nothing in life is forever. I can get through this." And the truth is, you can.

TWO

....

DREAMERS DREAM

I WAS CONSIDERED A DAYDREAMER IN SCHOOL. I WOULD SIT DOWN in class, listen to what the day's lesson consisted of, and before I knew it, the teacher's words would morph into "blah, blah, blah," and I would be off writing the most incredible story in my head. I didn't intend to mentally leave the classroom, but it happened pretty consistently.

Depending on the book I was reading, I would try on different personas and create an exotic tale of me traveling the world. I had a pretty good imagination because, at this point, I had never been on an airplane, traveled to a foreign country, or even heard a Southern accent. Sometimes I would go back in time and picture myself walking alongside a covered wagon out onto the plains or daydream about meeting up with Jo March in Concord, Massachusetts.

"Daydreaming" is often associated with derogatory connotations like "flights of fancy versus reality." It's used by authority figures, including parents and teachers, to describe someone who isn't paying attention, and should be. And if you're not paying attention, then you're wasting valuable time. This has to be when I started distrusting authority figures.

I got pretty good at faking my interest in the class. Or at least I thought I did. I'd try and not look too mentally distant, remembering now and then to make eye contact with the teacher. I did notice, however, that my teachers had a knack for calling on me when I was at the most dramatic point in my imagined story -- the part where I was about to do something really brave or even provocative. I'd have to quickly scan the blackboard for a clue to where the rest of the class was and try to make up an adequate response. While sitting by the window in Mr. DeBalso's math class, I found it extremely difficult to even feign a semblance of interest in geometry. When he called on me, I would say something like, "I'm really not sure how to do this exercise." I figured I could handle being thought of as a slow learner if he would only leave me alone to muse about things that really mattered to me. I didn't figure I would ever need geometry in my life going forward anyway.

The only time imagining is really encouraged is when an adult asks a child what they want to be when they grow up. You can go wild with this question and never get flack if you say "explorer" or "animal trainer" or "astronaut." The adults in the room don't really take your answers seriously anyway. They're just trying to get you prepared for the idea that for the next several decades, you'll be expected to plan out your life. You'll kick it off by having to state clearly on your college essay what you want to study and why. Who knows at 18, right? Four years later, you'll need a pithy answer when the human resource interviewer asks you, "Where do you see yourself in five years?" Good God, who knows!

As you've probably deciphered, I've never been inclined to plan out my life. I knew I wanted to write, live in the mountain, and always have a dog. I've managed to obtain two of said goals, more or less. When I was first married and living in Chicago, not anywhere near a mountain, I worked at a children's hospital overseeing communications. A young woman came into my office one day and introduced herself as an intern from the hospital administration program at the University of Minnesota. Before asking me about my career, she informed me that ever since she was a teenager, she had wanted to become a hospital administrator. Now, imagine my surprise. After all, who thinks of becoming a hospital administrator at 15 years old? I guess my upbringing in a small town was more of a detriment than I ever imagined. I'm pretty sure that as she was dreaming of hospital administration, I was drifting between a full-on fantasy life away from Mom and Dad and becoming adept at evading the security guards at a private estate near my house. My friends and I listened to music, drank beer, and smoked joints; plus a few other things we don't need to go into here. The only career selection we talked about was joining Chuck's band.

Anyway, as we chatted, the intern probed me about my career path while looking somewhat perplexed as I nattered on. After about 30 minutes of me spouting one upwardly mobile life point after another, she exclaimed that I reminded her of her brother. "Oh," I exclaimed, smiling, thinking this was the biggest compliment of all. "Yes," she said, "He's undirected as well." Since we were obviously living different lives with very different perspectives of success, the interview ended quickly after that comment. I did walk away from our conversation, however, thinking that she probably didn't spend much time daydreaming about other options for her life. In fact, I would bet my first child that she didn't waver from her life's goal and is now running a hospital somewhere in the Midwest. I only hope her hyper-focus paid off.

It's possible that I over-romanticize the benefits of daydreaming. But what if Picasso got stuck only painting still-lifes and never got to his Blue Period? We would be bereft. What if Thoreau didn't wander the edges of Walden Pond, and we never got to read his musings about nature? What if Ford thought horses were the best form of travel and the Wright Brothers didn't daydream about how birds fly? Where would we all be? Life would be pretty dull if we didn't put on our creative caps and stare out the window.

When my younger brother Stephen was about four years old, he was pretty sure he could fly. He walked around the house with a cape on telling all of us that he was going to fly to the top of the tree in our front yard. Now, most of us in the family either ignored him or made fun of him, depending on our mood. We didn't think he could fly and didn't think he really thought he could. Then along came a television show, "The Flying Nun," and he became convinced that if he had his very own nun's habit he would most definitely be able to take flight.

The premise of the show was that the novice nun, Sister Bertrille, was small, and the cornette she wore on her head with its long, side wings made of severely starched linen would lift her up in the air allowing her to fly. It wasn't magic. It was aerodynamics. Again, we ignored Stephen's talk about flying to his friend's house. Made fun of him when he told us he was going outside to fly around the house. But he wasn't deterred. He imagined himself up in the sky with a ridiculous nun's habit on his head. The talk then turned serious.

For Christmas, my little brother had only one gift request from Santa: a "Flying Nun" hat. He was sure Santa would drop one off under the tree on Christmas morning. My mother went into an all-out panic calling convents around the country in the hopes they had a leftover whimple in cold storage somewhere. Turns out the nuns are more frugal than sentimental and destroyed all of the "Flying Nun" cornettes so they could reuse the linen. Mom started frantically searching Simplicity patterns to make one herself. Only there weren't any patterns for a "Flying Nun" habit. Like a good mother, Mom was desperate not to disappoint her youngest and favorite child on Christmas morning. Three weeks before Christmas, however, she went into the hospital after a kidney stone attack.

Unfortunately for us, Stephen was confident and unwavering that his flight headgear would arrive on Dec. 25th, and wouldn't stop talking about it. My mother's friends -- one an artist, the other two seamstresses – watched the show and sketched the white linen habit from all directions and stitched it together. It was waiting for him on Christmas morning just like he expected. He wore it to the hospital to visit my mother and told her he would have flown up, but he didn't want to scare her.

The moral of this story is that dreams do come true. And ridiculous, imagined lives can make their way into reality. Or can they? Many of us at a young age thought about careers that turned out to be unattainable goals. Young girls who loved dance class dreamed of becoming ballerinas. And just about every young boy imagines himself as a professional athlete.

Imagining an alternative life is a way to feel good, get one of those natural highs, and think the impossible dream. Picturing yourself dancing across the New York stage can definitely bring a smile to your face. While daydreaming that you kicked the winning field goal is an instant ego enhancer for some. It's a perfectly wonderful feeling to daydream beyond your current existence. It's also a way to motivate yourself to go bigger, go higher, go for more in life.

I remember having dinner with a friend's father that was a genuine genius and an inventor. He spent the evening staring at the flame of a candle on our table, watching how the light flickered. Okay, he wasn't the most versatile conversationalist, but I was intrigued that he didn't even hide his daydreaming at a time when convention would dictate he talk to the rest of us. He had founded a company that created high-definition lenses for things like microscopes. He would take his imaginings and then create new scientific products -- all from daydreaming about light refraction.

For me, daydreams take the form of stories. For others, imaginings manifest into new products that change the way we live or work. Other people daydream about visual images that communicate ideas and concepts. And some people use daydreaming as a way to have a really good day. Daydreaming is a soul exercise, which to me, means it's a mysterious, creative, and expressive way of making sense in a world that, at times, feels dull and arbitrary. Daydreaming is a way to tap into the things we often keep private and safe from judging minds. It's a way for us to find our passions and what excites you about being alive.

We have to allow time throughout the day for daydreaming, however. Spending all of your time hooked to devices that constantly deliver bad news, cat and dog memes, and rantings on Facebook from your outsized social network detracts from spending quality time with yourself while you daydream. Some of my best times daydreaming were when I was riding my out-of-control Quarter horse with the wind whipping through my hair as we sailed along the old railroad tracks. I felt free and wild, and in control of my life, but never in control of Melody, my horse. I also loved to fantasize about what it would be like to live in the mountains as I stood on top of a ski slope, looking over the snowy valley and reveling in how magnificent nature is. I'd imagine myself living in a cabin, writing the great American novel. I often daydream while I drive, which I know is not kosher, and the reason I miss my turns so often. Mornings are also a favorite time for daydreaming as I sip coffee and think random thoughts. Spending quality time with myself in an unfocused, unplanned manner isn't a mission, neither is it a structured event. It's just an opportunity for me and my musings to imagine a storyline or think about what kind of dog I would want next or what it would be like to live in Costa Rica.

"Get your head out of the clouds," isn't a refrain I aspire to or one that I think is particularly useful. More than anything, I think we should spend more time in the clouds and less time being real. Daydreaming has been a gift in my life, taking me to faraway lands, creating business ideas that I could put into action, and picturing the type of family life I wanted for my kids. It was the kick-starter to so many dreams that ultimately came true.

I encourage you to get in touch with your early dreams. They surfaced either because you were interested in something or presented ways of working through overriding questions you had in your youth. Dreams can ground you when you can't find your way back to what you really want out of life. Daydreams, on the other hand, come to you throughout the day when your mind is still. They communicate passions, interests, curiosities, and life's meaning. Many women I counsel say they don't know what they want to do next, but after they've spent time reliving their past dreams and contemplating their present-day desires, there's usually a smile of recognition that shines on their faces.

....

THREE

CURIOSITY KILLED THE CAT

NICKNAMES ARE A WAY TO CONVEY INTIMACY. THEY'RE ALSO USED as a code for what someone thinks about you – sometimes they feel like a compliment, and sometimes they're meant to be offensive. Either way, they're descriptions of how other people see you. Our current president delights in conjuring nicknames to disparage people, but he's unusual in how often he feels inclined to name names. Luckily the nicknames I've been tagged with to date have been more perplexing than anything else and, possibly, somewhat telling about my personality. Both my uncle and my best friend's father used male names when addressing me: Stanley and Sam, respectively. I've never understood the relevance of either but choose to think of them as special names from two weird, older men. I would laugh when they called me by these names while raising my left eyebrow, which is a family trait for communicating, "You did what?" or "You said what?" I had no idea why they chose their nicknames for me. They never explained, and I'm still left with a feeling of total bewilderment when I think about it.

My father's nicknames were usually funny and revealing. He

called my sister Susan, "Noisy," due to her talkative nature. My best friend Betsy was "Newsy" because she could read the stock market at a young age. And I was "Nosey" because I asked so many questions. I'd say he was prescient because I've never stopped asking "why" my entire life.

There's really nothing more aggravating than a child who never stops asking questions, especially when you're trying to finish writing the last paragraph of a report after dinner, or you're desperate to get the bedtime story read and children to sleep. Unfortunately, many parents resort to the phrase, "Because I said so," as a way to finish the third-degree session.

To get an understanding of why things are the way they are, you have to read up on the topic in question, go to school and let teachers answer your questions, or lastly, try something out without all the necessary information and take the risk of falling on your face. I've tried all three to varying degrees of satisfaction.

I've always loved animals and felt particularly connected to most of the dogs I've owned. Saffron was a gorgeous Golden Retriever I bought when I was single and in need of unadulterated enthusiasm when I walked through the door. She had been trained by her breeder to do most everything I needed, so I never had to learn the basics of dog training. My next two dogs were babes in the woods, however, and it was up to me to train them. I did quite well training them to go potty outside and walk on a leash without pulling me down the street, but there have been two major fails – coming when they're called and crate training. I tried treats, changing my tone of voice, slapping my thighs, and other so-called training tips. I eventually had to rely on the fact that both my Spaniel and my Cavapoo were never going to have the look of recognition on their cute muzzles when I yelled, "Come." I would have to rely on them knowing they had a good thing going and wouldn't go far if they were off-leash at the park. I sold the unused dog crate at my last garage sale.

I absolutely did read books about dogs and how to train them. I spoke with other dog owners about my quandary and tried repeatedly to up my dog-training game. It wasn't a lack of curiosity about how to train them that derailed my success – it just didn't work. I don't ask "why" anymore.

Curious people use Google and YouTube a lot today. We used to read encyclopedias or ask our parents for answers to our questions, but don't have to anymore. We have IMDb to find out about our favorite celebrities, Wikipedia to look up geographical references, and YouTube for music videos or crash courses on how to fix anything. You could even make the argument that the more curious you are, the more time you spend on your devices. The only issue with this is that you may not always receive the best advice from Alexa or Siri. Also, the online world is fraught with inadequate and incorrect information, as well as stupid stories that people think are real. Just today, there was a story circulating on Facebook that Russia had let dozens of lions loose on the streets to enforce a stay-at-home edict during the global pandemic. Due to our gullibility and lack of fact-checking, most student assignment prompts explicitly state to be careful when using Internet research. The warnings don't matter, however, because we're basically lazy and will take a web article at its word. The Kremlin knows this to be a fact.

There are definitely cycles of curiosity as human development unfolds. Toddlers are curious about most things and take great pleasure in opening cabinets and taking all of the contents out. By grade school, many children have found an area of interest, which usually centers around socializing. As we progress in our development, we start to find our groove and begin doing more of it. I loved to read and escape into my fantasy world, only had a hard time finding a quiet place to do it in a small house with three siblings. I would lock myself in our one upstairs bathroom and tune out the repeated door kicks from my brothers to open the door. In fact, I got so good at tuning out the noise I can now read almost anywhere without headphones.

The downturn in curiosity begins in adolescence. At this point, our bodies and personalities aren't our own, and we spend our time obsessing about the body snatcher that has invaded our physical beings. Where we once were cheerful and full of zest, we're now dour and belligerent. Our curiosity extends to what our friends like to do so that we can feel like we're part of the group. Anything outside of the group is kept safely stored away for when we have private time.

As adults, our curiosities can be curious and often result in collectibles scattered around the house. Take Hummel figurines, for instance. Based on drawings from Sister Maria Hummel, a Bavarian nun, these porcelain images of children were introduced originally in 1935 to the U.S. market and sold by Marshall Field & Co., the Chicago retailer who is best known for Frango mints. Today, the figurines are celebrated at a national convention hosted by the M.I. Hummel Club, where thousands of members congregate to compare notes and prized possessions. There's even a museum in Illinois where a former mayor put his collection of 1,000 Hummel figures on display. I wonder how many people stop by the museum annually. Definitely curious about this.

In our house, curiosity often takes the shape of wondering about what goes on in a particular geography. My daughter has the most interest in traveling to new places, and during a particularly low period in college, taught herself the names and capitals of all 195 countries in the world. She would then time herself while she recited them from memory. I think her best time was under six minutes. Fortunately, her efforts have been rewarded, and she's been able to pair her cultural and geographic interests with a professional career. Sometimes our curiosity turns an interest into a passion. And sometimes the benefit of being curious is that we know a great deal about a particular subject. However, it doesn't mean anyone cares.

My husband is an avid fly fisherman. He's been fishing since he was a boy and often steals away for a few days to stand in rushing water and act like a bug so he can catch an unsuspecting trout. He then, of course, throws it back in, which makes the family suspicious of whether he's ever really caught anything. He's a card-carrying member of Trout Unlimited and, thankfully, recently found a group of colleagues who can talk shop for hours about fishing holes. His family is relieved.

On Father's Day last year, our daughter Anna thought it would be nice to do what Dad enjoys, so we all agreed to go fishing with him. We packed up the dogs and extra fishing gear and headed to the local river. We pulled into the parking lot and my husband quickly scrambled out of the car. He started rattling off all the different flies we would be using for the day. We didn't know what he was referring to and didn't bother to ask. He handed Anna a pair of waders that she reluctantly put on before trudging behind him into the cold, river water. Once she was standing waist-deep in the river, the bugs started circulating around her head. She took one selfie and then exclaimed she'd had enough. Out of the water, she took off the waders and handed them to our brooding son. By this time, the dogs were frolicking in the water and getting twisted in my husband's fishing line. He started swearing and, although I tried calling the splashing dogs to the shore, they weren't having any of it. Remember, they don't come when they're called.

After five minutes, my son put on the waders and went out into the water. My husband took this as his cue to start teaching Matthew how to fly fish. My husband likes to talk and teach and spent decades in a college classroom doing both. Our children learned at an early age not to ask him a question unless they were ready for a full-blown lecture on the subject. They usually came to me for a quick answer. After a few minutes of encouragement about how to cast, Matthew turned to his father and said he was done. I could tell my husband was crestfallen that none of us had any interest in fishing. His passion just isn't ours. We love that he has something in his life that keeps him curious and engaged. It just isn't our thing, and we can't even feign interest.

Information junkies are curious people. We love collecting data on a variety of subjects, and then more than anything, we like to relay this information to other people. Sharing about something we've read or learned is exciting and a way to connect with other people. Sometimes our sharing is appreciated and, other times, it's met with great sighs and eye-rolling. It depends on how the sharing takes place.

Passionate people can forget to look for facial cues that communicate whether or not the other person is interested in what you're talking about. If your information sharing is perceived as pontificating, there's a good chance you've lost the opportunity to get together again any time soon. In a business meeting, it can be overbearing when someone goes off on a subject in which they're trying to persuade colleagues to go in one direction or another. You know you've crossed the line when people in the room tune you out and start replying to their emails. Two things are going on here – delivery issues and content relevance.

Subject matter is deeply personal. One person's desire to know everything there is to know about gardening is another person's hell since the outdoors makes them sneeze whenever they set foot outside. Another person may like history and love watching war movies, which propels their spouse to leave the room as soon as the channel lands on a gory battle scene. One person may like reading the Classics while another only reads non-fiction. There are just so many varieties of subjects that pique your interest and no one else's.

We often gravitate toward people with similar curiosities as our own. My mother transcended housework boredom by joining groups of women in pursuit of similar interests. She was in an art club, a quilters guild, League of Women Voters group, bridge club, and many other group shares. Mom was always learning something new. She did well in these environments because she had the social finesse to participate and not get tangled up in committee dramas, like who was in charge.

Joining a special-interest group has been around for centuries. We've always gathered together to discuss what interested us. In the old days, our gatherings centered on the weather and harvest time. If we weren't interested, we wandered back into the fields to be by ourselves. Groups are just another channel for satisfying our curiosity. In many ways, it's better than sitting home alone surfing the web. Unless, of course, you're an introvert and people exhaust you, then the Internet may be the best option. The intimacy of person-to-person contact is needed at some point in your life, though.

Starting in high school, we're offered group options. They range from sports to music to academic areas of interest. Once we get to college there are even more groups to choose from. I was briefly drawn to the Young Socialists until I found out the FBI was following us around and taking photos. I wasn't that curious about socialism or that into the group leader I was dating to keep attending events. I also had peaked in high school with the group thing.

When I was a junior in high school, I joined a girls' sorority whose mission was to do good in the community. I mainly joined because my friends were interested, and I was curious about what the sorority did. I don't remember having any particular interest in being part of the group since the group thing has always been uncomfortable for me. I'm one of those introverts that can only take so much sharing. Anyway, we had to be asked to join, and then we had to pledge. Pledging meant they got to check us out before they committed to us being part of their group. Not sure why I would have set myself up to be rejected by a group of high school girls, but there you go. I felt pressured and did it. The last step before we were full-fledged members was Initiation. I didn't know what that meant since no one was allowed to share their hazing experiences with us newbies. We all met in a field near my house, and afterward, nervously walked into the designated wooded area. I remember thinking, "This is really nuts, and I wish I wasn't here." But I went anyway because I was curious.

When we got to the woods, the members were standing in a circle. They called us over and put blindfolds over our eyes. This is the point where you start cursing yourself for being curious. It's still hard to believe I actually agreed to participate in a hazing activity so I could do volunteer work in the community and have something to put on my college application. Seems extreme now that I think about it. The hazing ritual was fairly mild compared to what I've read about fraternity hazing in college. I didn't leave with PTSD or anything of the sort. They made us eat various concoctions that were vile but passable. Although, there definitely was some gagging and vomiting going on around me. Afterward, we all walked back to the road and said our goodbyes as newly minted sorority sisters. It was the last one I would join. My curiosity had definitely killed this cat.

Some of the things you try out of curiosity will indeed turn out to be one-time experiences. I ruled out roller coaster rides pretty quickly.

But other things, such as the taste of new and exotic foods can open up an undiscovered world for you. Have you been curious about anything lately? Did your curiosity turn into a new hobby? Or a favorite travel destination? Maybe you were curious to learn about a particular time in history. Or perhaps you're interested in trying out a new career. Curiosity can take you to places you've never been before and add a great deal of excitement to your life.

....

FOUR

MISPLACED WORKERS

THE WORD MISPLACED LITERALLY MEANS YOU'VE LOST SOMETHING, OR YOU'VE forgotten where you put that thing you're searching for, and now you're really frustrated that you can't find it. As we age, losing our marbles and other worldly possessions becomes a common daily occurrence. Before dementia sets in, it usually happens because we haven't yet learned Marie Kondo's organizational habits. We're just messy about our lives and the things we put in it. It takes years of practice to start making your bed in the morning or laying your keys in the basket by the front door, so you know where they are the next time you need them. It takes even more behavior modification to organize your tax documents before that April 15th deadline.

It's the worst feeling in the world to misplace something you value, especially if it's your self-respect and dignity. When I was eight years old, I joined the Brownies at my mother's insistence. I actually liked it after the initial push out the door since it was fun hanging with my girlfriends steeped in life skills learning and camping expeditions. Being a task-oriented person, I loved earning badges. Every year we had a presentation ceremony where we received merit badges for our new achievements. I was selected along with my next-door neighbor Paula to give a certificate of appreciation to her mother, Mrs. Wood, for helping us with our Outdoor Adventure badge. We rehearsed our speeches for days, then put on our uniforms and badge sashes and pranced over to McAllister Elementary School for the event. The auditorium was packed with family members, and I was becoming increasingly nervous because I had never spoken in front of a large group before. Little did I know that my appearance on this fateful day would be talked about for years to come.

When it was our turn, Paula and I walked up on stage with our hand-written speeches on rolled-up notepaper. Paula read hers to the audience and was flawless. As I sat in a chair off to one side, my legs started to shake. I could feel myself losing control with actual bats in my stomach instead of just butterflies. After Paula finished her speech and had stepped aside, I didn't move. I couldn't get myself up off the chair. She gave me one of those neck-jerk signals that connote you've missed your cue, so I awkwardly stood up, blurred vision and all. What I didn't realize was that my sash was hooked to the back of the wooden chair I was sitting on. As I walked to the podium, I ended up dragging it noisily with me. The audience started laughing, and I started laughing. I was laughing so hard nervous tears were rolling down my cheeks, and I couldn't speak. I tried talking once the audience quieted down, but every time I opened my mouth, I would break into peals of laughter and would have to stop. This went on for an eternity in my mind but was actually only a few minutes long. Totally humiliated and defeated, I finally turned to Paula and handed her my rolled-up paper and said, "Here, you do it." She rolled her eyes, exasperated, and read my speech. While standing next to her, I continued to giggle with a huge smile spread across my face in complete embarrassment. I don't remember who put the chair back.

To this day, my mother enjoys telling the story to new residents at her senior living center. My failed attempt at owning the spotlight at such an early age left me scarred and so unsure of myself that I couldn't even raise my hand in class to answer a question afterward. For years I got sweaty palms in team meetings if I had to present. Gratefully, I've gotten over my phobia and now enjoy a good showing.

It takes time to find yourself. It also takes some discomfort. At eight years old, I found that doing something new in front of a lot of people was tantamount to running naked down Main St. Over time, I came to understand the connection between believing in yourself and believing in your abilities. Success is an attitude as much as anything else. As an adult, I still get the jitters when it's showtime, but I have the experience to tell me that I won't shame myself again. I have the self-confidence to know I can deliver, but I wasn't there at eight.

We spend a lifetime trying to find comfort. We look for it in the places we live, the cars we drive, the clothes we purchase. We also find comfort in friends and family either because they're familiar or because we actually like being around them or both. Work is no different. The best jobs are those that we enjoy going to because our colleagues are people we like being around. When I joined an advertising agency called Draft, I found a whole cadre of people who made me laugh, which is paramount in my book, and were creative, smart, and really good at what they did. Because of this group, I looked forward to going to work. What a great feeling! A few years later, most of us, unfortunately, ended up leaving the company after a merger with another agency. Never believe a company memo that says a merger is taking place because cultures are so similar. Yeah, not so much.

I read a report the other day that concluded that almost 60% of the workforce isn't satisfied with their careers or their workplaces. How does this happen? Do people just take any old job and hope for the best? Do we spend less time contemplating our livelihoods than we do what PlayStation game we're going to buy next? Are our expectations way out of whack?

It isn't a coincidence when a majority of workers consider themselves misplaced. It's as though companies can't figure out how to match with the right employees, or employees themselves get lost along the way. The reality is that very few people have the luxury of waiting around until the perfect job shows up, even if you're self-actualized enough to know what that looks like. Just like finding your passion takes time, understanding what type of work fits you and where and who you want to do it with can take time. If you're an introvert, working in sales most likely isn't your game. And if you're an extrovert, working alone on projects from home and being human deprived will only add to the amount of Lexapro you need to take to maintain your equilibrium. Each of us has unique gifts and talents, and trying to be someone else just doesn't cut it in the long run. In fact, you'll misplace yourself.

I remember sitting in a job interview with a man who was so busy answering emails that he left me sitting in silence for over 20 minutes while he typed. I was desperate for a job because my business wasn't churning out any cash, but even in that state, I had the presence of mind to know that I should get up and run away. He clearly wasn't interested in me, and I wasn't impressed with him. He offered me the job, and I took it. I can say, unequivocally, it was the worst job decision I ever made – or at least in the bottom two. My new boss hadn't been forthright about what the job entailed, and the work turned out to be something I wasn't good at or interested in. Basically, it was a total fail, and I left after one year.

Finding a place that fits is the greatest gift in the world. The contrast is when Sunday nights fill you with dread about the upcoming

33

Monday morning. You sit on the couch unconsciously staring at the television screen, knowing that when you wake, you'll have to face the reality of your life. Now is that any way to live? Definitely a first-world problem, but one that reigns supreme for the 60% misplaced workers. For most people, it gets so bad that you don't even care if you're fired or have another job when you're ready to write your resignation letter. You just want out. I get it – boss man definitely drove me to a level of despondency I had never felt before. It was such a relief to never speak to him again. Even if it meant I was out of a paycheck.

Figuring out how to find that lost part of yourself is a winding, lonely path for most of us because no one else can answer what you lost and where it went. It's filled with "oops, not this" or "oops, not that" moments. The only way a reckoning comes about is by spending time thinking about what you like to do. If it was easy the majority of us wouldn't be working at jobs we found unsatisfying. It also has to be a priority.

Expectations for how to live have changed from one generation to the next. My parents' generation wanted to get home from the war, forget about it, and build a peaceful, safe life. They were delighted that you could buy canned vegetables that lasted for years in the pantry and new appliances to make cooking, cleaning, and mowing the lawn easier. The next generation wanted adventure, big mansions, and more of everything. As a Boomer, I can honestly say we missed the point of Woodstock. Doing what felt right definitely gave way to doing what made the most money. Our generation will forever be known for trading rolling papers for green paper.

Pursuing bundles of money is a passion for some people, but for most of us, it's a means to an end. After I got married to another artist, I decided it would be a good idea to leave the world of creative writing and pursue a career that would pay the rent and the grocery bill and, ultimately, our kids' college. I was being practical and felt very adult by making such a responsible decision. I applied to business school and got in, which was a complete surprise since I hadn't taken a math class in 20 years. I had already completed graduate work for an MFA, but now an MBA was the path of least resistance. After spending two years reading Latin American literature and writing short stories and screenplays, I was now figuring out algebra and contemplating Adam Smith's economic theories about capitalism. My husband almost couldn't sleep next to me because he felt like he was being unfaithful to his real wife.

Actually, I found most of my business program very interesting, but as a curious person, I enjoy learning about many subjects I don't necessarily intend to put into practice. During my first semester, I met my best friend in Business Ethics. We made eye contact as the class was debating whether it was ethical to manipulate the New York Times book review list for capital gain. We each nodded to one another as the conversation devolved into, "If it's not criminal, is it okay in business?" Lee and I became fast friends, and thankfully he was there to contribute to my passing grade for Game Theory and Probabilities. Second semester I understood about 40 percent of Derivatives and totally nailed Marketing and Negotiations.

There were a few key findings I made during my two years at Kellogg: 1) I realized I had never spent that much time with that many Republicans in my life, and 2) Business really is all about making money, and you have to care deeply about it to succeed. I thought I could make a go of it for my family. I spent several years after graduate school immersing myself in profit and loss statements, sales and marketing strategies, and even building new revenue models. Who am I?

Going from an MFA to an MBA was my left and right brains dueling it out. I couldn't commit to either one being dominant, so I decided a détente approach was best. I went into business and tried to rationalize my earnest desire to do good in the world by developing marketing messages that sold pharmaceutical products at highly inflated prices. As you can imagine, I had some internal conflicts about the career I had chosen. For me to be my best and do my best, and to feel energized and motivated, it's always been important that the work I do has meaning. I'm not motivated purely by money, so there has to be an intrinsic value in what I do for a paycheck that makes me feel like I'm contributing to society. Each of us is motivated in different ways. One of my classmates in graduate school sold plastic packaging and told me he was driven by competition and winning, so it didn't really matter what he sold. He enjoyed every minute of selling his plastic takeout dishes as long as he was beating his competition. I was definitely more of a misplaced worker in business than he would ever be.

Over the years, I tried different career combinations that married my interest in business with work that I considered meaningful. These included healthcare and marketing, startups that brought new patient technologies to market, and now writing and career coaching women. Once I figured out what motivated me to get out of bed every day, I was much happier. I've taken my left-brain knowledge and joined it with my right-brain intuition and creativity attributes to identify the most satisfying type of work for me. Phew! It was a crazy ride figuring that one out, and it's a great relief finding what I thought I had lost – me.

If you find yourself in a misplaced situation, it's not the end of the world. In fact, it's a moment to reflect on what would be a better choice for you at this time. Throughout our work life, most of us will have job experiences that ultimately don't fit well, but don't despair. The best part of living in today's world is that there are choices and pathways forward. Ask yourself what it is that you like about your job and begin discovering potential industries, companies, and positions that allow you to do more of it. I recommend, though, that you make a decision to find a better position than the one you're unhappy in. It's empowering to make choices that are good for you. You get quite a self-esteem boost knowing that you're taking care of yourself.

FIVE

BIG AND SMALL WINS

EVERY NOW AND THEN I BUY A LOTTERY TICKET. I'M not sure why because, in all my years of sporadic trying, I have never gotten one number correct. In fact, I have never won anything from a game of chance. The only kind of luck I've ever had is with cards. During junior high school, Mom and I used to play fierce, gin rummy games on the back porch during summer vacations. She never let me win, so I worked hard to learn the game and figure out her tricks and weak spots. I'm something of a gin rummy champion in our family now. My brother thinks its luck, but since I have no other evidence that I can win without working hard at something, I think there's mainly skill involved. I do love to win, though.

Actually, we all love to win. It makes us feel special. There are also many different ways to win: first place in an athletic event, the top prize in a spelling bee, Miss Universe crown, Nobel Peace Prize, a coveted sales contract for big bucks, the top pick in the NBA draft, and a lot of other ways that take you to the top of the class or an ac-ceptance speech at a podium. You can win the lottery. You can win a trip. You can win at love. The options for finding a place of winning in your life are enormous.

There are also ways that winning doesn't really look like winning – the kind that comes from a diabolical need to take all the winning spoils for yourself at any cost to you or others. Napoleon, the one and only emperor of France, comes to mind when I think of a way to win that ends up costing you more than you won. However, I doubt that when he was exiled to an island off the coast of Africa, the power-hungry and insecure military wizard spent much time contemplating where he went wrong. Did I overstretch at Waterloo? Should I have relaxed the rules of the Royal Court to have more loyal fans? Perhaps if I hadn't abdicated my throne things would have worked out in my favor. And then to reassure himself, "I did win for a really long time, though." Napoleon ended up spending his final six years on a rock island, alone, possibly being poisoned but definitely suffering from stomach cancer.

Without naming names, we've all witnessed personal triumph that came from plowing over everyone or living outside the margins and taking the goods by any means possible. The criminal element is saturated with these folks, but so is Corporate America. However, there are also winners whose hard work and dedication to a craft, art, sport, business idea, or life concept made it inevitable they were going to make it to the top. In his book, *Outliers*, the author Malcolm Gladwell talks about how successful people, called experts, actually spend over 10,000 hours in pursuit of their goal. I'm pretty sure Michael Phelps spent way more hours than that in a pool. And Simone Biles must have spent an infinite number of hours on the balance beam to get it so right. She didn't get 25 world titles by being a slacker.

Individuals who pursue excellence and then win in their area of expertise are on a mission to be their best and do their best. As audience members to their individual achievement, we give them accolades and rewards. We write about them because they inspire us to also be our best. We're in awe of them because, as mere mortals, there's not a chance in hell we could accomplish what they did. Why? Because each of us has our own goals and our own definition of winning, and it won't necessarily result in an Olympic medal. Winning requires focus and a recognized end game. Even winning the lottery requires you to buy a ticket. And winning at love means you have to go on that blind date.

This is where winning gets tricky. When I was in a graduate writing program, I worked for one whole year on the same short story. It was tedious trying to get it right, but then I learned that Scott Fitzgerald took 50 tries at writing *The Great Gatsby* introduction, and I felt like I was in good company. When the two years were over, and I had finished the program, I packed up my short story in a manila envelope, tucked it into a moving box, and there it sits to this day. Was it a waste of time? Did I fail because I didn't publish the story? Learning how to write fiction was a personal development goal of mine, and finishing the graduate program made me feel like a winner. There was no public congratulations or outward sign that I was going to become a great American fiction writer, but my sense of accomplishment made me feel special. It also made me feel like I had invested in me becoming my best -- a winner.

There are many outward signs of winning, but even if the wins are only seen by you, they're still important to creating a life well-lived. You may not get a pat on the back for acts of kindness or sticking to your values of being a person who lives their life with integrity and honor, but these can feel like personal wins as well. Not everyone is driven to become a doctor and cure cancer or learn Python software code and start a tech company, but does this mean you're a loser?

Does winning always have to have big, audible signs of recognition to call it winning?

When a woman decides to leave her lofty and high-paying career to raise her children, does she think, "I'm winning" or "I'm a loser because I can't figure out how to do both well?" Her kids grow up and become productive members of society who pass on the confidence, support, and love they received from her. She feels it was worth it for her and her family. Obviously, in this example she wasn't raising her kids alone, or she would be working and raising kids at the same time. But let's pretend we all have this choice. The point is she defined success and winning in her own terms.

I remember when my mom encouraged me to sign up to become a Rotary exchange student. I hadn't really thought it through but figured why not. It could be fun living with a strange family in a strange country and surviving puberty all at once. After I applied, I had to go and publicly state to a Rotary panel why I wanted this opportunity. However, my classmate was more convincing in her answer and got to pack her bags for Brazil the next year. I felt ashamed that I wasn't chosen. I wasn't the top choice, and it made me feel insecure and inferior, which are two good reasons to only go after the things in life that you really want to win. I didn't really want to leave my friends and venture out into the world at that time. I definitely did later, but this was more my mother's idea than mine.

I've had to learn the lesson of projection as a mother as well. Just because something sounds worthwhile to you doesn't mean it's great for your kids. I always loved rock climbing and being outside. Every Saturday, I brought my two children to an indoor, rock-climbing facility. My daughter would scramble up the side to the top with no trouble, always ending the day with a smile on her face. But my son would get about five feet off the ground and let go, swinging in the air until the instructor caught him. I learned later that my son has a significant fear of heights and hated every Saturday we went. So much for apples falling close to the tree.

When I entered the business world at the age of 23, I wasn't sure how to win. At that time, there weren't any textbooks on how to work your way up the corporate ladder, only show and tell opportunities. Some people did it by being emotionally intelligent maestros who knew how to work the internal political game and find a path forward. Oftentimes, this was done by attaching themselves to an older mentor, which didn't work as well for women as it did for men in those days. Some employees moved upward by being the best singular contributor in their area, which was great for them, but unfortunately for the rest of us, they often stayed until retirement. This left little room for other staff to move up the corporate ladder. And then there's another type of employee who lied, cheated, and slimed their way forward. Some things never change.

I worked for one of those people at my first company outside of publishing. She was pleasant and didn't get in her team's way, but then again, she didn't engage with any of us either. One day I walked into the office, and there was police tape all around the filing cabinets and across her doorway. The staff members were huddled in an office whispering and called for me to join them – nothing like a little police scandal to pull a team together. They informed me that our fearless leader, who had been with the company for over 20 years, was a complete fraud. She had a different "real" name and was embezzling about $20k a month through a phony vendor company. As you can imagine, I couldn't have been more surprised. Now, what do you think? Did she win? It sure didn't look like it from the side of the glasshouse I was sitting on.

A few months later, a Board Member from the same company went to the local newspaper to proclaim that the Chairman of the Board had sold the company out from underneath everyone. The company was a non-profit, multi-hospital system that the Chairman had created from scratch. The accusation was that he was negotiating with a for-profit company about an acquisition without keeping the board informed. It was an election year, and as you can guess, the board member was a Democrat, and the Chairman was a Republican. Even back then, healthcare was a hotly contested issue. At the risk of going out on a tangent here, it's 2020, and we're still having the same conversation about healthcare. Looks like another problem left for GenZers to solve.

The final outcome of the board accusation was that the Chairman resigned and filed a $10 million defamation lawsuit against the company. We all went into crisis mode, and I ended up spending 16 hours a day fielding media requests and managing the communications for the company. After months and months of having no life, only work, I burned out and left the company. Good first job. Learned a lot. Not sure who won.

At the end of our life, people often take stock of their lives through memories, storytelling, photos, memorabilia, and grandkids. It's too late to take back the failures, and the wins are past memories that no one wants to hear about anymore. For most of us, our wins come in the form of how we feel about our life. It's true, a large bank account would be a nice affirmation of success, but for the 99% of us who didn't get the latest tax break, our Social Security benefits will have to suffice to pay the rent.

Wins in life represent moments mostly. They include the time and effort they take pre-win, then the actual win, and then the follow-on adrenalin high post-win. The pre-win effort takes either the 10,000 hours of learning how to do something well or finding ways to carve out the opportunity where you can succeed. Most of the time, you have to really want something to win at it. You have to be committed and energized because being your best takes focus and effort.

I'm going to go out on a limb here, but to me, a lasting win in life isn't about a career choice, but one where people I love, admire, laugh with and carry on with are all at my table. Throughout our married life, my husband and I brought people into our home to share what we have and for us to become a part of their journey. To be welcomed into someone else's life is a gift and an honor.

I'm grateful for all the wins in my life, both big and small. I like the feeling of being my best and doing my best for myself and others. I'm also grateful that most of my wins didn't cost other people anything. And I'm truly sorry for the wins I had in my life that were at the expense of other's aspirations, goals, or self-esteem. It's better when everybody wins.

Don't forget to celebrate the big and small wins in your life. Make a list of your recent wins and pat yourself on the back. Find something to reward yourself with that gives a nod to your achievement. It's too easy to only focus on what isn't working in life as we strive for perfection. If we look for it, we also find things in our lives that are working and bringing us joy. They make us feel like winners.

SIX

TIME PASSES BY

I DON'T KNOW ABOUT YOU, BUT I SURE WOULD LIKE TO take back the minutes, hours and days that I've wasted over the years and can't ever get back. It's not that I believe I have to be productive at all times, but I can certainly think of a few periods when I was definitely not making the best use of my time. Watching *The Bachelor*, for instance, or some other inconsequential television program comes to mind. Or wasting time doing something I feel obligated to do but don't really like doing, such as cooking dinner. It's just not in my wheelhouse of talents, and my kids will vouch for me here. They still make fun of the time I burned a balsamic reduction and made the house smell like tar.

Knowing where to spend time for the maximum return is akin to becoming a self-actualized person on Maslow's hierarchy of needs. It requires a good bit of old-fashion soul searching. You can't possibly become acquainted with your intentions, passions, and purpose on the fly. However, how and what you spend your time on matters – this isn't an equal opportunity exercise. Spending hours alone in your office telling yourself you're indispensable while others are out enjoying themselves isn't really quality time. It also doesn't necessarily represent productive time or an investment in your future, especially if you're left haggard, resentful, and isolated. In fact, many leadership experts suggest the most self-actualized people spend more time being distracted and unconsciously working through problems in the zone than begrudgingly sitting in an office with their head in their hands. In other words, you can sometimes get more accomplished by sleeping, taking long, luxurious showers, or hiking in nature than staring at the same problem for hours on end. I understand daytime naps are big in new tech companies.

I once reported into a client who was the very essence of a workaholic. I don't think he ever left his office and, consequently, was grouchy most of the time. He barked orders, was suspicious of his employees, and seemed agitated whenever I spoke to him. I met his boss one day while out walking on a golf course during an LPGA tournament and was told that my client had been fired. I was shocked since I assumed he was a valued employee because he spent so much of his waking life on the business. This was before I understood what self-actualized meant. After I stated my surprise to the CEO, he said, "Yeah, I always wondered why he never wanted to go home." Hmmm, guess he wasn't solving the right problems for the company.

Work is something we do, usually for someone else, and to make a living. It represents only a part of our lives, but a significant portion of it. Work takes many different forms from executing tasks to conceptual development, but without passion for what we're doing, it's tedious and hollow. Being passionate about what we spend most of our waking hours on brings into play an emotional response to what we're doing. Passions are creative outlets that allow us to express connection, love, worth, and meaning. If you're lucky, you're passionate about your work, which will drive you to overcome obstacles and move your project or business forward. Passions give you a reason to care about what you're doing, so work becomes visceral and exciting. Being passionate also makes work time feel like speed dating – your days fly by.

After I finished graduate school, I tried my hand at several different jobs, but I kept coming back to the same thing – I need to find meaning in what I do, which is why working in healthcare fit with my passion for doing something with my time that serves other people. I've always seen healthcare as a bellwether sign of how well a society is serving its citizens and a front-row seat for assessing how well our communities are providing what people need. While I was working in China, I witnessed the point in the country's economic development when people went from simply surviving to concerned about their quality of life. Chinese citizens had lived with scarcity for a long time and, therefore, didn't have the luxury of thinking about longevity or wellbeing. When jobs became available, and business opportunities opened up, hospitals started building cancer centers and cardiology suites to help people live longer and better. It was amazing to watch. A byproduct of China's growing middle class also included citizens buying luxury goods and skin care products in mass quantities, but I digress.

My passion for helping people took me into the entrepreneurial world where I built a digital company to help people with the cost of healthcare in this country. Have I mentioned how much luck and timing are part of building a successful new company? Well, I entered the startup world as an entrepreneur during the 2008 financial crisis. It was also the time when the Affordable Care Act was taking shape. It's now 2020, and I find myself building an executive coaching business for women during a global pandemic and massive layoffs. Needless to say, my heart and passions are in the right place, but my timing is consistently out of whack.

Focusing our attention, time, and money on a passion is not without merit, even if the end result is bankruptcy. Yes, I keep telling myself this, but in my heart I know it's true. Living a life of passion is very different from always playing it safe and never exploring whether you can have both. Not everyone has the opportunity or support system to take a flier late in your career. I could have been much more reasonable and figured out my passion while at a job, but after the company I was working for was sold, I decided to try and build a company. It had always been a dream of mine. Sounded reasonable and very exciting at the time.

We spend so much time at our jobs that work often becomes our life. It's where we find like-minded individuals and even, sometimes, deep friendships. It's also a place to explore sides of ourselves we weren't aware of by taking on projects or teamwork outside our comfort zone. It's also the place where we can find inspiration or even paths to unearthing talents long dormant. This is the best that work has to offer.

When my daughter was three years old, our nanny suddenly moved back to Ireland. My husband and I were desperate to find a school placement for Anna. She really wanted to be around other kids and not stuck at home with another adult all day. Chicago is like most large cities where school placement is hyper-competitive, and the seats are in short supply, especially for pre-school programs. Who knew? Not this small-town girl, that's for sure. The Chicago French school was brand new and was looking for students, so we were fortunate to get her registered right away.

Very early into this experience, we realized that Anna had a talent for languages and a strong interest in culture. However, we questioned our decision to help our child become bi-lingual after her first full sentence in French was "You eat like a pig." Our family vacations were usually spent traveling in our Dodge minivan to Ohio to see her cousins while many of her classmates were ex-pat families going home to France or South America for the holidays. She was intrigued and asked for a globe for Christmas her first year at the school so she could see where her new-found friends were from. Now, not everyone has identifiable interests from a young age that later track to a career. Anna found her way to a career path that uses both her language skills and her passion for learning about people who are different from herself. My son's Legos fetish hasn't translated quite as smoothly.

The ability to combine work and passion is a gift. It's also a way to live a fulfilling life that, at its core, offers meaning and purpose. Unfortunately, it takes time to become self-aware enough to know how to put your life together in a way that feels directed and authentic. It's very much trial and error as well as dedication that you won't stop until you know for sure what you want to spend your time on and how you want to spend it. Finding what drives you is uniquely yours, though, since this information comes from past experiences, ingrained beliefs and values, and proven loves. People today are finding that sitting in front of a computer for hours on end in a sterile office isn't their cup of tea. They prefer telecommuting where they can walk their dog at lunchtime and dash off to an exercise class right at 5 p.m. And up until the global pandemic, the gig economy was providing a lifestyle and wage alternative to hooking up with corporate America.

Choosing how we spend our time is a luxury for many people, but it can take the form of making small choices that reinforce that we have some control over our lives. It can be as simple as choosing who you spend time with and what you do when you're together. I've sworn off being around toxic people, which means I have to pace myself with the news. I can only read stories about politicians every so often. Knowing that you have choices is empowering, and I recommend taking advantage of it as much as possible. Pass the time with certainty and purpose. Grow your garden and weed it mindlessly and with pleasure. It's your time, after all, to spend as you wish.

Section II

Living On An Emotional Rollercoaster

Steep climbs and fast drops make life a daily hazard, but what other choice do we have? We have to keep going! Learning to change our perspective about being uncomfortable, and not afraid to edit out what we don't want, provides moments of great clarity. No one said we had to like rollercoasters.

....

SEVEN

NEVER TOO OLD TO FAIL

FAILURE...SHMAILURE...WHATEVER. IF YOU'RE NOT GIVING YOUR LIFE A RUN FOR its money, you haven't accepted the rules of the game. How else are you going to become a living guru by the time you reach retirement age? After all, a life well-lived is one that plays the percentage game and bets on a few failures and a whole lot of satisfaction.

I no longer believe that life is about minimizing failure. After one particular pity party a few years ago, I realized that my inability to create a multi-billion-dollar business would not be my last failure in life. In fact, it has become clear to me that if I continue to exist on this planet, I probably will have a few more spectacular failures to live through. That is if I choose not to wall myself off from other people and experiences.

Tripping over life's fallen branches is inevitable. Some of these failings might be considered unwise choices or even unsuccessful tries, but however you categorize them, they often hurt your pride, ego, and self-respect, and sometimes, even your shoulder, back, and head. Brushing off failure as "I didn't really want it anyway" is just window dressing so that the outside world sees a well-adjusted, mature person. Inside, you're a two-year-old toddler throwing her Barbie doll across the room in a fit of rage. It just hurts not getting what you want.

As parents, we should ensure our children understand that they won't always grab the brass ring even though they've put all their heart and soul into finding it. And don't start the conversation by telling them how you had to walk five miles to school in a blizzard. As parents, we want our children to know how much harder it was for us to succeed than it will be for them, which usually results in a bored, ho-hum look thrown our way. A good lesson for our kids, though, is to be told that trying is just as important as succeeding and then mean it. If you don't try new things, you never get a chance to grab that ring. The strange thing, though, is that we all get lots of kudos for going for it, but when the result is less than stellar, everyone looks away – like when you fell down during a missed pitch at a company softball game.

As adults, we forget that from an early age we are conditioned to try uncomfortable things with no guarantee that we'll like where we land. Remember trying to learn how to walk? Yup, lots of bruising along the way. Learning how to form words and articulate a need and then later a point of view -- frustrating as anything. One day I was driving my daughter and young son to school, and he was trying to tell us something that was on his mind. The first time he said it, my daughter and I looked at each other and shrugged our shoulders because we hadn't caught one word of what he was saying. I asked him to repeat it, and he did. Nope, didn't get it the second time either. Lovingly, I asked him to repeat it again. He tried again. My daughter and I quickly became squeamish as we couldn't decipher a single word he had said. I asked him to repeat it again, and he shouted clearly, I might add, "I hate you guys!" and folded his arms across his chest and stared out the backseat window. It felt awful witnessing his failed attempt to communicate with us and seeing the misery on his cute, little face. The good news is that his speech improved over time, and we can now understand him perfectly. Of course, he's 20 years old.

We have lots of ways of talking about failure in our culture. Failure is most commonly defined as an unsuccessful completion or an unmet end result. It can also mean "fiasco." None of these definitions work, however, when you're talking about "failing health" unless you had it written into your life plan to live way longer than your body concluded is in your best interest. The definitions work pretty well for the term "failed marriage," which is usually associated with fiascos and unsatisfactory end results. As I scan the celebrity gossip rags at the grocery store checkout, I'm often reminded how uncool it would be to have your personal fiasco on public display. You can almost always read a headline about infidelities and irreconcilable differences that cost millions of dollars to finalize. These stories are usually paired with cringe-worthy photographs that are definitely not photoshopped and are the ultimate visual for showcasing a fiasco of a failed marriage. I'm grateful to be a nobody and that my failures will never be front page.

As a country that thrills in other people's misfortune, there are many ways we talk about failure, such as lost time, which refers to wasting time. A quick example would be when you're being too self-critical and call out how "You're losing time to find the right partner, or a high-paying job, or better path." What you're telling yourself is that the actions you've taken so far haven't been useful, and you're blundering around losing time to get what you want. An example of wasting your time might be the innumerable people we know who have spent thousands of dollars getting a law degree, and then decide in their third year of graduate school that they were never, ever going to practice law. From this side of the decision, it could look like a waste of time and money, but most of these people went on to forge careers in business, investment banking, federal and state public policy, and other careers that consider knowledge of the law an asset. Acquiring more education has rarely been a waste of time.

What failures really should be called are "attempts at trying something new." How else are you going to collect all the necessary information you'll need to decipher if you're in the right spot, with the right person, and doing what you should be doing? My sister is a therapist and often reminds her nieces and nephews that the 20-something decade is when you should try everything! When done with caution, it will definitely take the pressure off for when you're older and not getting the results you want.

I enjoy watching younger people try and figure things out. You can literally see the "aha" moment when they realize that maybe a different decision along the way would have saved them the excruciating pain of not doing something correctly. Either that or they just need to bear witness to a failed attempt to collect more data. Over the years, my husband and I have hosted numerous young people in our home who were either studying locally or interning at Chicago companies over the summer. Young people bring vitality to the lives of older people, and we, in turn, offer wisdom and experience to the younger set.

When my oldest niece and her future husband lived with us, my husband found a willing and able sous chef in Ryan. They're both foodies and could talk all night about the vagaries of certain types of yeast. It bored my niece and me to tears. One day, Ryan decided to take the lead on dinner since my husband was still at work. He's a charitable guy who isn't afraid to step up and take charge. He also knew he'd starve if dinner was left up to his two female roommates. I was reading a book on the patio when he came outside to start the gas grill. He lowered the lid, turned on the gas, and then ignited the gas starter to light it. Low and behold, the gas exploded, and Ryan was left with singed bangs and almost no eyebrows! Luckily, that was all that was blown off. Sometimes lessons are more severe than anticipated, but as you can guess, Ryan never made that mistake again.

I've attempted many different things during my life and gathered a trove of information on a variety of subjects. Some data I've collected will never be used again, such as adopting a child from Vietnam, or renovating a rundown 1890's house in a city with lots and lots of construction codes. I spent hours on both subjects: researching best practices, interviewing other people who had gone before me, and endlessly talking about the next steps with my husband. I was traveling unchartered territory, attempting to figure out subjects that were frightening and uncomfortable. Happily, the house turned out beautifully, and from the moment I met my son, I knew that he and I were meant to be together. Love them both dearly.

One attempt I'm conflicted about is starting my own digital company in 2008. Yes, the same year the financial crisis blew up, and everyone's 401k's went kaput. I had always wanted to work for myself and enjoyed the art of creating something new in most of the jobs I had held. Because I had a habit of developing new products, departments, and divisions for companies I worked at, I had the resolve to give it a go. After the company I was working for was sold, and my role was eliminated, I decided the time was right. I even talked a few colleagues from different old companies into participating in the enterprise. My partner and I raised money from friends and family and hired a technology team. What we didn't anticipate was that the entire medical insurance industry would go into convulsions, and we wouldn't be able to pivot fast enough. I was there for six years and used all of my savings and retirement money to keep it going.

Before you shed any tears (believe me, I've shed enough for both of us), you need to know that I'm telling you this story because it has a high degree of failure associated with high levels of learning about being an entrepreneur. We've all heard the Facebook, PayPal, and Amazon stories. Let's just suffice to say that hard work, luck, timing, capital infusions, and big *cajones* were involved in their success. Intellectual brilliance may or may not have been a critical factor. I won't judge.

I had been to graduate school and done well in the Entrepreneurship class. By the time I kicked off my own startup, I had worked at three digital startups – two failures and one successfully exited. The reality is that sometimes there just isn't any substitute for being in the middle of an experience and seeing first-hand what it really takes to build a company from scratch. Reading about it and not being responsible for paychecks was no substitute for being the executive most accountable.

My fact-finding expedition was painful, embarrassing and financially unproductive, but I was in good company. More than half of all startups don't make it. Since then, I've parlayed my learnings into helping other startups develop products, assess their market potential, and mentor leaders. It could have been a disaster and, was for a while, but the final result is that I'm one heck of an informed entrepreneur with lots to give – even if it's only a shoulder to cry on.

This is probably a good time to also note that my marriage hit a wall during this very stressful time. Everyone deals with stress differently, and the resulting effect is that it can cause damage to even a good relationship. My husband had left his teaching position and wasn't able to find another job during the financial crisis, which only added to our financial woes. He withdrew, and I stopped sleeping. It took some time for us to find our way back together.

One of the things we learned was that before we could really function as a couple again, we needed to forgive ourselves and each other for the situation we were in. Never before in our relationship had we had money worries. We had experienced other types of concerns, but none related to finances. This was new to us, and we were ill-prepared for the havoc it reeked on our family. When a partnership hits a rocky road, it's useful to look at what the issue means to each of you separately. Money is one of those issues that can wreck a home. It's usually because one person needs more of it than the other and puts more value on how much is in the bank than the other person. We've both had to learn to live with less money in savings and to be okay with it, while not blaming the other for our predicament. Forgiveness is key to moving forward.

For whatever reason, this attempt at starting a business was what I needed to do to add to my investigation about how to live fully. I no longer regret that choice. You've probably got a few of these bright-eyed ideas in your own back pocket as well – bunging jumping in New Zealand, joining Cirque de Soleil, becoming a pilot, a parent, an investor, or a first-time dog owner. You may want to move to a foreign country where the language, food, religions, and government are different from your own. There are endless options for what you might try in life. Regrets are the worst, so I wouldn't recommend them as a way to exist in this life. If you give something a try, and it doesn't work out, learn from it, and move on. Shed your humiliation and pride and embrace your humanness and willingness to fail. Perspective and attitude are both keys to living an enjoyable life, even if your life experiences have been marred by bumps and bruises along the way. You'll always be in good company on this front. Now go out and fail and have a good life!

EIGHT

SEEING IS BELIEVING

PEOPLE HAVE ALWAYS NEEDED TO BELIEVE IN THE MAGIC AND mystery of life – the power outside ourselves that influences how well or poorly we live. Grappling with life's mysteries also helps us make sense of the world around us. This deep-seated need to figure things out, label, and then formulate a fervent belief is very much a human thing. I haven't observed the animal kingdom relying on a worldview in order to operate. It's pretty much: eat, sleep, and play. Doesn't seem like they care about the "why."

Religion and politics bring out the most passionate beliefs, so much so that when I was growing up, I was told, "Whatever you do, don't discuss who you're voting for or what church you go to." Various religious beliefs have explained how the world works for centuries, actually, since the beginning of time. For the majority of people, religion provides a sense of protection, guidance, belonging, and knowledge to its followers. Suffice to say, many of us need to believe in the unseen to soak up the hope that a helping hand is available when we need one. One reason we look to outside guidance or the inner self in prayer is that religious beliefs help to explain why we're here and what purpose being alive on Earth serves. It also gives us glimpses into how humans have survived over the millennium. It would be too much to ask, though, for the planet's 7.8 billion people to agree on the why's and how's of life. We'd rather fight about who got the right signals from above than give up any ground. It's amazing we've lasted as long as we have.

As a young girl, I would sit with my family in the pew of our local church and sigh heavily during the sermons. They were long and tedious, and I wasn't so sure that what the priest was saying was true. In other words, I wasn't sold on his explanation of who God is and what he wants from us. There also was a lot of sitting, standing, and kneeling sequences that I found annoying during the one-hour service. While I lived with my parents, I went to church dutifully every Sunday and didn't skip Sunday school until I was in high school. In my younger days, I mourned not being allowed to stay at school and do art projects like my Protestant friends. Instead, I was shipped off with the other Catholic kids to St. Helena's church basement.

Among other things, religion is a metaphor for how we see our place in the world. It provides us with a worldview from which to live our lives. You can see how visceral our need is to understand the mysteries of life by observing young people. When my sobbing niece asked her mother where her pony went after it died and was hoisted by a crane into the back of a flatbed truck, my sister tried being vague and comforting. She told her kindergarten-aged daughter that the pony went to where all good animals go—a place called animal heaven. Sara Beth looked at her mother incredulously and said, "That's the dumbest thing I've ever heard."

Different religions tell different stories about how the Earth began and who is in charge. For the most part, we grow up aligning with a particular religion based on which one we're introduced to by our parents and religious leaders. As adults, we come to realize that, besides religion, there are many other beliefs we accumulated in early life that influence our perceptions about the world around us. These beliefs revolve around education, health, government's role in society, genders, different cultures, nature, among other things. How we come to embrace our beliefs varies, though. For instance, sometimes, we embrace beliefs because they're *simpatico* with what we want to believe. Another reason is that that they're derived from observations that we see as factual and, therefore, true. And third, our beliefs can be developed from what another person we hold in high regard tells us to believe. A belief system becomes the foundation from which we operate and is central to how we see the world, including ourselves, other people, and institutions. They also serve as our internal meter on how to interpret what we see, feel, and experience. They tell us what is true.

Beliefs are contextual and experienced as our "truth," which explains why most of us are extremely passionate and protective of our point of view. They also serve as the basis for why we hate, fight, and separate ourselves from one another. Deeply held religious and political beliefs have caused the most wars. It's as though these beliefs are only valid if you're protecting them as either a warrior or missionary. Exhausting, really.

Beliefs are derived from both emotions as well as facts. For instance, I believe that if I were to try driving on the left-hand side of the road in England, I would be at risk of a head-on collision. This isn't an emotional belief, but rather one based on knowledge about my driving skills. This belief will probably save my life someday. Now my belief that my adorable Cavapoo won't love me if I don't give him daily treats is totally emotional with no facts to back it up. Many of our emotionally derived beliefs are shaped by childhood relationships.

One such belief, "I believe that I'm a good person," is a feeling you have about yourself that comes from your parents telling you that you're the best kid in the whole world. This didn't really happen, but let's go with it. It also comes with a prescribed moral code that dictates you care about other people and exposes you to the revelation that the world doesn't revolve around only you.

The conflict occurs when you believe something and act otherwise. For example, as kids, I was forever leaving my sister stranded in trees that she was too scared to climb down from. I was an expert tree climber and way too impatient to wait her out. I even left her in the gigantic maple tree in our side yard one day, sweating out her descent until my father came home for lunch. She must have been up there for at least two hours. The good thing for me, however, was that despite my actions, my sister has always been my best friend. I'm very grateful that forgiveness is part of her belief system. Marrying up beliefs with actions can sometimes take time.

Because our worldview creates the way we walk through life, if you believe that nothing good will ever come your way, it may not. If you think you don't deserve the best in life, you may never try for it. If you believe you're too dumb or too unskilled to get the job you want, you won't get it. We project our worldview onto everything we do. It's easy to spot someone negative and insecure. It's just as easy to notice someone kind and wise. Helping us come to terms with our worldview has also been a boon for therapists and the pharmaceutical industry.

The interesting thing about worldviews is that they can change. You can go years believing that Santa Claus distributes presents to good children on Christmas Eve. After all, your parents told you the story, and the presents always appeared under the tree. I loved believing in Santa Claus. It made me happy. He made Christmas special.

And then, one day in third grade I overheard classmates talking about Santa not being real and poof, my worldview about the payoff of being a good girl for an entire year was gone.

The hardest part of changing your worldview is that it feels like you're losing a piece of yourself. You see yourself and your life one way, and then something happens and, it's like a veil has been lifted from your eyes. The biggest headbanger for me was believing that everyone had the same chance to succeed in life, and then walking into the real world in the late 1970s. I didn't like finding out that it wasn't true for women, people of color, immigrants, and other non-white males. I had to replace my naïve worldview with one that worked better, one that would prepare me for the obstacles I would face as a woman in the workforce.

For a while, I found that my idealistic belief system was replaced with an angry, cynical world view. I joined a newly formed group called the National Organization of Women comprised of women who were also tired of running into structural barriers at work and were, rightly so, angry about it. The problem was that my newfound reality was a total downer. For my sanity, I had to find a way to evolve my worldview to allow for hope and positivity while remaining realistic about the world I lived in.

I had grown up in a small town where we didn't discuss the world out there. Instead, we folded up into ourselves and celebrated life through community picnics, Little League games, and friendly neighbors. I, of course, had heard of John Kennedy, Martin Luther King, and Bobby Kennedy, but they didn't really touch my life. I didn't feel their struggles or fully understand how civil rights, Vietnam, and women's rights were being played out. It didn't affect me until it did.

Slowly, I replaced my idealistic beliefs with a belief system that centered around the individual and what each of us can accomplish on our own. It allowed me to take positive steps toward becoming the person I wanted to be and building the life I wanted. I could no longer believe in society as a support system for my dreams, but I could believe in myself. This newfound belief system was a shocker, however, and reverberated through most of my ideas about the way the world actually works versus how I wanted it to work.

As a girl, I was taught that only thinking of yourself was selfish. After all, women needed to care for their husbands, children, and community-at-large. We weren't supposed to linger in our own dreams — we were the cog in the wheel of other people's lives. This is still true for most women around the world today. It just so happens that in Western countries, over the past several decades, we've been able to push through to create a modern view of women. We've been able to carve out a place in society, and in our own lives, that gives us the room we need to explore, succeed, and create. There's a reason that women like Eleanor Roosevelt and Ruth Bader Ginsberg are icons in our pantheon of heroic women — trailblazers who helped bring us all along. Although, there's still a lot of change that has to happen before the modern woman is fully realized.

Finding a worldview that works for both you and the society you live in can seem like you're working at cross purposes. In other words, if it's good for me, is it good for others? I, personally, don't accept a world where only a few people thrive. My worldview is that I'm responsible for my life and all that I put in it. I also understand some of us have more opportunities for exploring "my view" than others. If you have it, then take it but don't use it as a hammer on others.

My belief about personal responsibility was cultivated early on but was expanded soon after I was married. After our wedding, I moved to Chicago to be with my new husband since he was up for tenure at a local university and wasn't as mobile as I was. I left all of my friends and my beloved East Coast behind to drive to the Midwest to begin my new life. When I pulled onto the Skyway Bridge leading into the city, I burst into tears. I was afraid that I had left all the good parts of my hard-earned life behind. I was fearful of what lay ahead; I wasn't concerned about who I had married, but I was unsure what being married would mean to my life.

In the first few months of our marriage, Craig was working days teaching at the college and nights directing a play. I was left alone in our apartment with no friends or job and was becoming increasingly bitter. This was not how a new wife should be treated! I felt that I was supposed to be cared for and nurtured as I found my sea legs in this new city. Instead, I was lonely and miserable. Then one day, as I was thinking about where my white knight was, I realized I had walked into the fairy tale trap. The story was really about a woman who wanted to relinquish control of her life. Is this what you do when you feel inadequate about managing your own life? As I sulked and walked along Chicago's beautiful lakefront, it came to me that it wasn't up to Craig to make me happy and fulfilled in life. It was actually my responsibility. Oh, and I so wanted it to be his job! After all, sometimes it's just easier to let someone else take the lead. The downside to giving up control of your life is that you have to accept where your partner is driving the bus, which requires a whole lot of trust and acceptance. At that moment, I saw that the institution of marriage was not meant to make everything in my life okay. I realized that it was only going to be okay if I made it that way. Strangely, I hadn't even realized that I had this worldview – being a feminist and all. Somewhere in the back of my brain, I saw the pairing of two people as a way to dissolve my individual responsibility for myself. I guess I thought marriage was going to be the safety net that let me off the hook.

I grew up around women who weren't "modern." Almost all were married with children, which is what women did in those days unless you joined a convent. Some women worked outside the home, but many didn't. And only a few had college degrees. Those who did were teachers, guidance counselors, social workers, and secretaries – all classes of helpmate. Unfortunately, not all women were fulfilled by the tasks of motherhood and marriage, which was obvious by the screaming coming out of their open windows. My belief system about marriage and womanhood grew out of years of observing these women. They were singularly connected to family life in a way that made them disappear as individual women. They had become their assigned roles. For the most part, these women had nice homes, clothes, and cars, but who were they? I have no idea. Were they happy? Probably some of them were.

So obviously, I had subconsciously incorporated my observations of Sherrill, NY, family life into a worldview that said, as a woman, you get subsumed as soon as you say, "I do." I didn't consciously believe this nor did my husband. The result of this realization was that I had to come to terms with this lurking worldview and get a hold of myself. I had to change my beliefs about marriage and, more importantly, women in marriage, which allowed me to be an individual separate from my husband while also being a partner to him. Didn't quite know how to do this, though. No role models for this kind of change.

The first part of breaking down a belief system is to become aware of the parts of it that no longer work for you. The second part is to actively design a new one. This is where therapists come in, as well as good friends. I started asking girlfriends how their marriages worked. I also had the benefit of having participated in the women's movement in my 20s when many women were vocally fighting for the opportunity to change society's worldview of the role of women. If you've seen the television series, *Mrs. America*, you know not all women were on board.

What transpired after I realized I was waiting for my husband to rescue me and be my hero was a sense of emancipation. I knew that I would be happier if I dictated what went into my life and didn't succumb to tradition. I also knew my relationship with my husband would be happier. So, I started building an unprescribed marriage where we took care of ourselves while also nurturing one another. We also meted out family responsibilities based on what each of us liked to do and not on traditional roles. Consequently, I haven't cooked in almost 30 years, and Craig stays out of most of our celebration and vacation planning. We each get to be the individuals we want to be and do the things that feel in keeping with who we are. It works for us.

Over the years, my beliefs about religion, marriage, parenting, education, and health have all been overhauled, thereby editing my worldview. I didn't set out to undo my deeply rooted beliefs, but as I developed and observed the world, my old belief system didn't work for me anymore. It's been a relief to shed some of the old beliefs, as well as a struggle to let go of others. Each time I opened up to new information and ways of being, I became a better version of myself. I think I also became a bigger, more expansive version of me.

In order to find a belief system that works for you, you have to learn to really listen to others and see how they live, work, and partner. Sometimes we get our backs up when we're confronted with different opinions or ideas, ready to duke it out for the right belief. But I know that when I've been open to new ways of viewing the world, I've come away with a deeper understanding of what I believe and why. My ability to "see" life around me has been a motivator to develop beliefs that serve me better. Our worldview is a projection of who we are and where we've been, like a reflecting pool that shows you scenes of how you're interacting with the world around you.

NINE

....

EXPECTED RETURNS

THERE ISN'T MUCH WE SET OUT TO DO IN LIFE that we don't expect to find a golden nugget in the end. I'm pretty sure I wouldn't have bothered with college if I didn't expect to graduate with a diploma that gave me the ability to hunt for a low-paying, low-level first job. After the first job expectation was checked off, most of what I've taken on over the years has helped fulfill the probability that I would have a successful career. I cultivated benefits that rewarded me for my efforts and got me closer to the expectations I had set for myself.

The truth is that most of us are more interested in outward appearances than trudging on for the sake of exploring our personality and inner self. For the most part, we don't work on toning our abs because we're enlightened human beings. We do it because we want to look amazing in that new bikini. It's only after your life doesn't unfold the way you expected that you begin to exam your expectations about life. By the way, very few people have their lives unfold as expected, so don't despair. The good news is that surprise happenings bring out the hot and spicy seasonings of life.

Your first expectations are set early on by other people. In our family, there was an expectation that we would someday move out of the house and stop asking my father for money. He says he found nirvana when he could get on a telephone call with one of his four children and not reflexively reach into his pocket for cash. Other expectations were that we would go to college, stay out of jail, and live good, honest lives. Happy to report that all of us have met our familial expectations. I didn't stay home and become a high school English teacher, though, so I disappointed in that account.

Besides family, expectations are also set for us by teachers, government leaders, religious leaders, and anyone else that serves in an authority position over us. These are the people that show us how to live within the rules they abide by and want to hand down to the next generation. They teach us how to make accommodations so that we are part of the mainstream flow similar to how the movie, *The Stepford Wives*, portrays suburban women who have perfected being good wives. The thinking is that if we all march to the same drummer, we'll live comfortably within our communities and not stir up any trouble – think housing covenants and house colors.

So, what happens if you decide to set different expectations for yourself than the ones handed to you on a silver platter from a young age? I'm not suggesting that I would have wanted to stay on my father's payroll any longer than he wanted me to, although it would have been nice to linger there for a few more years than I did. What I am suggesting is that maybe going off to college at 17 wasn't the right answer for me at that time. I had no idea what I wanted to study and didn't take my classes very seriously. Now you understand why graduate school was in the cards for me. For undergrad, I chose a university far away from New York State in order to start from scratch, where no one knew me or expected me to be what they wanted. It was an odd way to choose a school, but what I was really interested in was traveling and seeing the world. Whenever I could scrape together a few dollars, I would set off for Mexico or somewhere else I hadn't been before. My enjoyment came from scanning a landscape I had never seen and trying to make sense of it. I came to expect that this would be a big part of the way I lived my life.

It's conceivable that my rebellious streak sprang from growing up in the remnants of the most successful utopian, religious community in the United States, which was not a mainstream role model. It was called the Oneida Community and was first established in 1848 by John Humphrey Noyes, a rebel divinity student from Yale. The Community was buttressed between the small towns of Sherill and Oneida and had expectations that were very separate and distinct from the local communities. The Oneida Community members called themselves Perfectionists and lived off the tenants of personal enrichment based on God-endowed gifts and talents. In other words, there was an expectation that your Earthly responsibility was to hone your talents, often pursued through formal higher education for the men, and without the confines of an exclusive relationship or child-rearing. Their belief in free love, as you can imagine, was anathema to the locals' conservative Christian beliefs. Actually, it's surprising they weren't run out of town like they were in Putney, Vermont. Besides not marrying, they also didn't raise their own children. Adults rotated through the communal Children's Home to guide and care for the young ones. After being quarantined for several months during the COVID-19 pandemic, I believe most parents would give rave reviews to the idea of communal parenting. Zoom conference calls would be considerably less interesting, however, but probably, more productive.

For most of us growing up in the Sherill/Kenwood area, the Perfectionists were a source of pride. They had achieved something way outside the confines of normality, which ultimately ended in a successful joint-stock silverware company and created a societal community that thrived for more than 30 years. Being a Perfectionist was no picnic, however. The name alone pretty much sums up the rigors of adhering to the Community's beliefs and expectations. Being a perfectionist myself, I can attest to the dark side of always trying to do and be perfect. It keeps me from participating in arts and crafts and is one reason I detest sewing -- the clothes always look handmade, and not in a good way. The Perfectionists held public criticisms in the big hall where a member was taken to task for not bearing up to their end of the bargain or meeting the Community's expectations of godliness. The purpose was to "eliminate undesirable character traits," such as selfish love. One fellow brought before the Community was a man named Charles Guiteau who, ultimately, was rejected by the Community. He left, got into politics, and later went on to assassinate President James Garfield, whereby he was hanged for his crime. We don't talk about this much.

As parents in charge of expectation setting, we can't help ourselves – we project onto our children what is important to us and then expect them to see the world through our eyes. Both my husband and I chose to go to graduate school, he then spent most of his life teaching at the college level, and we both have always believed deeply in being curious and maintaining a lifelong learning posture. However, our son has pretty much always hated school and made a point of letting us know this in very creative ways, such as when he barricaded the principal in her office at his Montessori school. He struggled to get through high school and spent one miserable year at a community college before he decided to take a break. It terrified me that he wouldn't have a piece of paper to help him find his place in the world. I had thought that setting an expectation for our children that they would graduate from college was a given. It was not.

It seems a bit crazy now that my expectations took me to a place where I believed there was only one way to be successful in life. Raising children is definitely one of the best ways I know to be forced into a reconciliation of how your expectations affect other people. If I didn't have two strong and determined kids who made me take a look at my expectations of others, I may have gone through life judging and expecting everyone to make the same choices that I had made. There are still times when I think they'd both be better off if they did, however.

Being challenged about your expectations is a painful stab in the heart. I didn't know how to help my son navigate the world he was entering and was frightened for him, or maybe it was me I was scared for. Luckily, he approached looking for a job with gusto and got a job in the restaurant business. The global pandemic then hit, and the world became even more uncertain for people without college-level skills. What has happened, however, is that I'm learning to let go and resettle expectations that I've set for others. I'm trying to step back and let my son create his own expectations for his life. This is such new territory for me. Part of my role in the family is to make sure everyone is okay. At least that's the role I've come to expect for myself.

It's so disappointing when people don't adhere to the expectations you've set for them. The funny part about this is that our family is pretty much comprised of rebels who rarely do what others expect of us. Having Matthew be a part of our family has taught me so much about being present in the moment and releasing the unfounded responsibility that his life is my life. Our son has helped me realize that everyone has the right to develop their own expectations about how they're going to live their life, within the confines of not hurting other people in the community, however. We all expect that.

Creating your own personal expectations about your life is often seen as being in direct conflict with the community-at-large. Why? Because we all want to parent everyone else and set expectations for others. Let's not confuse expectations with legal rules that bind communities in health and wellbeing. Expectations are ways that we as a group push conformity, and if you rebel against these expectations, you're considered weird, unfit, and sometimes even an outcast.

I'm always impressed with people who don't care about being seen as weirdos, nerds, and outsiders. Take gamers like my son Matthew and his friends, some I know in person, and others are online friends I've heard about. These are young people and some older who basically sit in their rooms all night, slashing zombies and talking with strangers through a headset. It's become big business and devotees take it very seriously. Because of the large numbers that participate, I wouldn't call them outsiders, but they definitely are paving their own way. No parent that I know of set the expectation that their son or daughter would be a gamer. It's not that we object, it's that we're ignorant about what it all means. I have to say, though, this particular community was probably the most prepared for a global pandemic. In fact, I'm not sure they even realize we're having one unless, on the off chance, they needed to step outside for one reason or another.

As a society, we've been pretty consistent in our struggle to parse out the rights of the individual versus the broader community. We're constantly going head-to-head on divisive and politically charged issues. Lately, we've even witnessed people take up arms and threaten others with violence. We've become a society locked into endless arguments about your expectations versus my expectations. Some people try to win by sounding the alarm of moral and religious codes of conduct, but we know that's not what these issues are really about. They're about who gets to set society's expectations. They're about locking down "my way."

There are so many societal expectations that it's hard to keep track of them. Some are as trivial as what manners you need to use when eating in good company. My mother was a stickler for table manners, so I grew up knowing which fork to use when. It was paramount in my house that no one ever asks if I grew up in a barn. To this day, I'm uncomfortable watching people who fumble with tableware decisions. I feel embarrassed for them because I know they'll be judged. Knowing the difference between a salad fork and a meat fork doesn't seem that important, but in some circles, it will communicate that you're not meeting the basic expectation of what manners look like. Sounds silly, right?

Setting your own expectations for your life is courageous. It's especially brave if they are against the mainstream. When I was right out of college and working at a magazine in New York City, I met a very nice older man who was a senior editor. It was a small staff, so we had ample opportunity to get to know one other. One day he confided in me that he really didn't like his job very much. I was intrigued that he didn't get up and walk out. When I asked him why he stayed, he mentioned he had a mortgage. At first, I wasn't sure what this had to do with him staying in a job he didn't like. But he went on to explain that he felt bound to care for his family and not jeopardize being able to meet his financial obligations. I was struck that he viewed this job as the only way to be responsible for his family.

When you're young, you see your life as having unlimited possibilities. As you age, it can seem like your choices are more limited, which I guess is where my colleague was at. After our conversation, I told myself that I wouldn't live a life that was only attuned to financial obligations. Having said this, I did set an expectation that I would always ensure my family was well cared for and had what they needed. This didn't mean that I always chose how to make the most money at my own expense. To this day, it still makes me sad to think that my colleague expected life to be a win-lose proposition, trading his personal joy for his family's security. I truly hope he figured out how to have both.

Experts recommend that you should set realistic expectations in order to have some possibility of them coming true. It's as though you have to do a personal inventory of your limitations before you can confirm you've identified achievable expectations. The alternative, I suppose, is to set expectations that ultimately send you into a death spiral of disappointment. This thinking of setting achievable expectations, actually explains why so many people follow expectations that others set for them. It can seem less risky.

Expectations are not the same as setting goals. Goals revolve around an action plan while expectations set out needs and what you want. For example, I expect to be thinner by summer because otherwise, I'm never going to the beach, which could be realistic. But if I said, "I'm expecting to look younger by summer," then I will probably be disappointed. Now to figure out how to reach my expected weight, I have to put together a plan of action and set goals. I guess it's time to research Weight Watchers again.

Whether you're setting your own expectations or someone else is doing it for you, expectations are a part of everyone's life. Running away to Arizona helped separate me from pre-determined expectations, but eventually, I had to devise a new set for myself. You can't hide from expectations, but you can change them and make friends with the idea that there are things you want to do, to achieve, and to have during your lifetime. So, what are they?

TEN

THE SCARIEST CLIMB OF ALL

'VE LOOKED FEAR IN THE FACE MORE TIMES THAN I can count. There are times it's smacked me hard before I either ran away or punched back. I'm no Jack Ryan, but neither am I Kevin Hart squealing at the sight of a llama. For most sane people, fear is one of those things that you'd rather hide from than face. I have heard, though, that entertainers and athletes tap into their fear and anxiety before a performance to get the endorphins flowing. For most of us, it's a sign that a major panic attack is brewing.

It's not hard to describe what fear feels like – heart palpitations, throbbing headache, shortness of breath, and paralysis in the extreme. Defining what our fears are about can be more difficult, but most of us suffer from both irrational and rational fears. I never understood why my daughter didn't like being held. Then, one day, we walked into a crowded elevator, and she started pulling on her trachea and exclaiming, "Mommy, too close." It was then that I realized she was claustrophobic and not just stingy with her hugs. Hugging her is like putting your arms around a hard, wooden telephone pole.

Other people are afraid of insects, flying in an airplane, getting shots at the doctor's, or even going outside. I, for one, am afraid of bears. This may seem irrational to you since I live in a dense, urban city, but when I was a kid, I used to go camping in the Adirondacks with my best friend Betsy and her family. Every single time a black bear would saunter into our campsite, I'd feel the blood drain out of me. Just the thought of being attacked drove me into a state of utter panic and geared up my nervous system for a whopping flight response. By the way, you should never try to outrun a bear. You can't. The fact is that black bears are generally opportunistic about foraging for food, which doesn't dim my fears at all. They'd much rather nibble on leftovers in a garbage can than human meat.

My irrational fear of bears has pretty much kept me from touring some of our more beautiful national parks. Never in a million years would I be inclined to hike or camp where there was the smallest threat of running into a black, brown, or grizzly bear. I can't even bear the thought. As an adult, I participated in one family camping trip, again in the Adirondacks, with my sister and her family. The first night my husband left a pound of chocolate fudge he'd bought in town on the picnic table. An entire family of well-fed raccoons showed up in the middle of the night for a celebration. When I unzipped the tent flap to see what was going on, the mother growled, and the children sneered. I was uncomfortable knowing they were out there, but I wasn't covered in cold-sweat fear.

After a day of torrential downpour and trying to keep a two-year-old occupied in a soggy tent, I went into town and begged the reservationists at the Marriott Hotel to find me a room. It was summer, and they were all booked. I gave her my mobile number and pleaded with her to call me if something opened up. Luckily, a family left early, and I was able to secure a hotel room that everyone in our two families wanted in on. The following morning, I opened the curtains to take in a view of Fourth Lake, and to my surprise and utter dread, there was a large black bear ambling along the lake's edge. Earlier he had been spotted going through the hotel's garbage bins. This was the last time I went camping.

Unfortunately, fears keep us from doing certain things in life. I really would like nothing more than to be able to invest my vacation days in exploring Yellowstone National Park. It's not going to happen, however, because the entire time I'd be riddled with an irrational fear that one of the more than 700 grizzly bears in the park would try rolling me over with its four-inch-long claws after I dropped to the ground in a safety tuck. Therefore, the closest I'll ever get to seeing this natural wonder is driving through the park's paved roads with the hope that I don't hit a bison along the way. Maybe hypnotherapy could help.

The opposite of an irrational fear is one that you're very sure merits a deep abiding distance from. As a city dweller, I can think of several of these, such as staying away from identified gang territories, avoiding dark alleys where rats forage for food, taking public transportation at rush hour, and leaving your car in a no-parking zone. It's perfectly reasonable to stay away from all of these. I would also stay away from various things in rural areas of the U.S., including driving on no-shoulder country roads covered in ice, taking a walk in a field with a no trespassing sign hanging from the fence, chasing tornadoes, or calling myself a feminist in a crowded room.

Rational fears usually come from experience, either yours or someone else's. They are based on factual accounts that make your life better if you heed their warning. This seems as good a place as any to talk about novel viruses. When we first heard about COVID-19, we weren't sure how dangerous it was. But then, after China sprang into action and closed down an entire city of 11 million people it became quite obvious this wasn't a virus you wanted to catch. At first, our country's leadership believed our concern was irrational, but after the virus landed in Seattle, New York City, and on Carnival Cruises killing people at a rapid rate, it was evident that this virus was more than the common cold or seasonal flu. We then started seeing political, medical, and governmental movement to try and contain what appeared to be a dangerous new illness. The word "novel" does mean you don't know anything about it, which is one reason to fear it. And if there's one thing I know about myself, it's that doing anything the first time makes me uncomfortable, and often, fearful. So, we all became fearful about a new virus that can attack your lungs and suffocate you to death. Sounds reasonable that we got our flight and fight responses churning in overdrive.

Anything you do the first time sends shivers through your body. Firsts are the scariest because there isn't any information to help you navigate the situation. Wearing masks has been done around the world for years, but it's new to the U.S. Infectious diseases aren't new, though, think polio, HIV/AIDS, SARS, and Ebola. As we learn more about a subject, fears lessen. Hopefully, our emotional reactions to this pandemic will coincide with scientific data and identified treatments, and eventually, a vaccine. In the meantime, our country will seesaw between fear and calm as we open up the economy and begin interacting with one another again. What a relief it will be when we have a better understanding of how the virus works and no longer have to classify it as a new fear.

We all have to overcome many different kinds of fears during our lives, such as driving a car, leaving home, interviewing for a job, matching on a social dating app, buying a home, having a baby, and maybe even starting a business. If you can remember what it felt like when you plunged in and did these things for the first time, filled with trepidation and fear, you can use the cellular memory of white-knuckling to your advantage. I often remind myself when I'm trying something new that I have survived first times many times before.

For me, the scariest climb I ever took was committing to marriage. You may scoff at this, but let me tell you, I didn't see it coming. By the time I met my husband, I had pretty much decided I wasn't ever going to get married and have children. I had had several decent relationships, so it wasn't that I had given up on the idea of love and partnership. I just couldn't see myself spending decades with the same person.

A commitment of any kind was frightening to me. It requires you to come to terms with "yes" in a way that feels confining and boring. I wanted adventure, changing venues, and reinvention to be central in my life and didn't see how marriage could offer me this. I also always wanted an out. Now, marriage isn't a new concept, so I had ample information and observations to draw from. I even took a marriage class in college for an easy "A" elective. The professor spent most of the class talking about systems management and how to set up a successful system with your intended mate so that you wouldn't have to try and change it later, such as the way you communicate or spend money. The supposition was that you knew what you wanted and how to devise it at the onset. I don't know any married people who had the foresight to get it right from the beginning.

Commitment anxieties are most often rooted in personal history. I didn't know this at the time because I thought I was pretty clear-eyed about relationships. What didn't occur to me was that my choice about staying single was rooted in fear. It's so odd that you can see yourself as a survivor and not realize the toll it has taken on you. The reality was that my parents had a marriage I didn't want to replicate but wasn't sure I could avoid.

I met my husband at the one place I never thought to look for a date – a funeral parlor. I happened to be friends with an older colleague at work whose husband I knew only fleetingly. He passed away after a long illness. I showed up at the wake to pay my respects and standing before his father's picture was a good-looking young man. We started flirting right there in front of his dad. I went over to my friend Lois' house with another friend after the wake ended, and Craig and I talked and talked into the night. After we left the house, my other friend mentioned how sensitive he was, to which I reminded her that his father had just died. I wasn't terribly impressed that he had an emotional side at this time in his life. Now here's the surprise of the century; a month later, Craig came back to Boston from Chicago, and we had our first date. We had two more dates before he proposed, and about a month later, I said "Yes." Yep, never saw that coming.

Our connection was obvious to everyone around us, even to me who can be somewhat obtuse on matters like this. I was 33 and had long ago been able to determine if a date should be during the week or had the makings of a weekend date. I didn't want to waste my weekends if I thought we wouldn't make it through dinner before our attraction dissipated. And here I was now, considering a marriage proposal to a man I had just met and barely knew.

My sister Susan and her family came to Boston for a visit and met Craig, who was visiting from Chicago. While she and I were alone in the kitchen, I meekly told her that he had asked me to marry him. She asked what my response was going to be, and I said I didn't know yet. She then called me a coward. Now, this is remarkable for two reasons: First, she's a therapist and rarely, if ever, is this forthright about her opinions, and; Second, she knew Craig and I had met only six weeks earlier. She obviously also knew that I had a commitment phobia, and was in need of some prodding. Anyway, it was the jolt I needed to get me thinking about whether I was going to let this man go. It didn't take long afterward for me to say "yes."

In some ways, the decision to marry Craig is consistent with my impulsive nature to just do it. Nike would be proud. In a span of a few months, I had gone from being fearful about committing to anyone to being excited about starting a new life with a relatively unknown partner. My instincts were right, however, and after decades he's still the kind, generous, and funny man I thought he was.

One of my takeaways about fears is that it doesn't have to take a long time to overcome them. Even if a particular fear feels deeply ingrained, it can be dealt with swiftly if you decide to push through. Taking lots of deep breaths and positive self-talk also helps. Fears hold you back and burden you with historical baggage that tells your brain to be anxious and scared when confronting a particular scenario in life. They're not your friend. Turns out, my marriage is nothing like my parents', and I was right to take that scary climb. I can't imagine what life would be like today if I had succumbed to my fears about entering a committed relationship and stayed single. I would have missed out on so many loving, humorous and adventurous moments shared with a person I consider my best friend. I also would have missed out on the opportunity to learn how to push through tough times in a relationship, which is a lesson worth learning.

Do you know what scares you? What will it take to move past your fears and get uncomfortable so you can try things that might be good for you? Facing your fears means not letting them get in the way. It doesn't mean not having any. What is one action you've always wanted to take but didn't because you were too scared? Today is a good time to stop letting negative thoughts get in your way and begin doing the things on your bucket list.

ELEVEN

··

PROMISES

Starting with "pinky swears" on the playground, promises are a way people establish bonds with one another. "I promise to love you forever." "I promise to always have your back." "I promise to make pizza for you every Friday night." Some of the more prominent promises come out of religious teachings that guarantee us a place in heaven for upholding the ten commandments, including honoring thy father and mother and not committing adultery. As a Catholic family, we also made a promise not to eat meat on Fridays. Granted, not as big of a promise as one of Moses' commandments, but it did require us to order fish fries from the American Legion every week. In hindsight, this doesn't feel like such a big lift, especially if you like fish, which I do. Anyway, commandments and religious rituals are big promises to keep. But we also make smaller, every day promises to stay in touch, be on time, pay our bills, and take out the trash. Promises build trust between individuals and connect us as intimates. These connections make us feel safe and secure, well, most of the time.

I once had to promise my mother I would pray for patience. She put me in the corner facing the wall and told me to start praying. I faked my promise and spent the time making ugly faces at her behind her back. In my teens, I also had to promise never to shoot up marijuana, which was the easiest promise I ever made to my parents.

When you make a promise, it's usually expected that you're sincere about it and trustworthy. A mortgage broker processes your loan because they believe you'll pay the mortgage amount every month for the next 30 years. When you sign a confidentiality document, you're promising to keep silent about the matter at hand. And when you adopt a puppy from a shelter, you're promising to neuter the pet asap.

What makes a promise so extraordinary is that it's a commitment to another person given either in writing or verbally. Before social distancing, promises were also sometimes accompanied by a handshake. In today's wacky world, however, we seem to be in an alternative universe with everything said and promised is tagged as "fake news" or cloaked in a conspiracy theory. It's shaken us to our core and makes it hard to know who to believe or what truth really is. So, what happens in a society when giving your word is no longer trustworthy? If there's no repercussion for lying on camera and then saying you didn't say it, or when you can sign a legal document knowing full well you have no intention of fulfilling your promise. Does this mean we're done with the phrase, "I give my word?" Do we just do away with promises and bonds to one another? Do we accept living in a world where we can't trust one another – ever?

Lies are used sometimes to get out of promises. Most of the time, these are little white lies about why you're late for work or why you couldn't do your homework. I've definitely lied about liking a gift my husband gave me as well as telling him I was feeling fine when I wasn't. But these weren't promises, rather lies to cover up true feelings I didn't want to admit to. When lies are used to get out of promises, such as treaties, contracts, covenants, and engagements, you've taken lying to a whole other level. You've broken a trust that has much bigger consequences than telling someone you're a few years younger than you really are.

Most of us aren't in the position of breaking huge promises that can affect national security or relationships with allies. For us, lies result in breaking down our personal and professional relationships, and cause hurt and disengagement. It feels awful on both sides. For many of us, the worst breakdowns happened as teenagers when we promised our parents that we would behave ourselves while out with friends. It felt pretty awful to try and sneak back into the house after missing a curfew and have one of your parents sitting in a darkened living room waiting for you. It wasn't that you felt bad because you were late, but rather because you got caught and now would have to pay the price. They felt bad because they couldn't trust you to do what you said you would.

I haven't broken a lot of promises in my lifetime because I try and only make ones I'm sure I can keep. I've kept confidences, been there for friends, and kept promises I made to colleagues. I don't make promises to people I don't trust. I want my word to mean something, so I try not to get entangled in situations where I feel compromised – like promising to lie for someone or promising to help someone do something illegal. It may sound like a low bar, but I've been able to meet it over the years.

As caregivers, we're asked to make difficult promises about upholding a parent's quality of life when they can no longer make their own choices about medical care. A few years ago, my mother sent each of her children a copy of a living will that she had found in the personal ads of a local newspaper. It was the size of a small label and needed a magnifying glass to read, but basically, it gave us the responsibility to take her off life support if we deemed it appropriate. You could vaguely make out her signature, and it may or may not be considered legal when we need it. The promise to do what someone else wishes at the end of their life is one big promise. It's also essential that you trust the person you're giving the authority to carry out your directive.

This is one tough promise for families to make, however, because your idea of what constitutes quality of life may be different from what is stipulated in the living will. My father never had a living will because he wasn't convinced we would know when he was at the end of his life. He used to say he didn't want us, "pulling the plug too soon." I've given up trying to decipher that level of mistrust from him. It's not like he was leaving us a fortune or, even a penny, that we couldn't wait to get our hands-on. As a lawyer, he must have seen his share of quarreling families and decided to beg off entrusting his life to his spouse and children. We didn't ask about his clients, and he didn't tell.

In addition to promises we make to others, we also make a lot of promises to ourselves, such as being a responsible parent, dedicated employee, or good neighbor by not leaving your children's trash in the front yard for weeks on end. Most of us tie our aspirations to promises to ourselves about what type of life or career we're going to have. I once promised myself that I would never work for "the man," but quickly realized he paid well. I also promised myself that I would spend every winter on a ski slope, but then married a man who didn't ski. I also live in Chicago, which is 323 miles from the nearest hill driving east and 1,000 miles from the mountains of Colorado.

The importance of a promise may fade over time. When you're in the heat of the moment, you feel completely sure that the promise you're about to make is one you will keep. But maybe after you made the promise, you quit that job or lost that friend, and the promises you made to them no longer seem important. Are promises meant to be kept for an entire lifetime? You tell yourself that there's no harm in telling a secret now that you no longer see that particular person. You find yourself in a moral dilemma because you badly want to tell the secret. It's a big, juicy story that you're dying to share. It's probably time to bring back blood promises that produce scarring so that you never feel inclined to share a promised secret, no matter how long ago you made the promise. One look at the scar and you're chastened.

When immigrants come to this country, they come for the unspoken promise of a better life. I know my grandparents believed in this. Afterall, inscribed on the base of the Statue of Liberty is Emma Lazarus' sonnet, "The New Colossus." The most well-known lines from her poem are, "Give me your tired, your poor, your huddled masses yearning to breathe free, the wretched refuse of your teeming shore. Send these, the homeless, tempest-tossed to me, I lift my lamp beside the golden door!" It pretty much promises a welcome mat to those who want to enter this country, and most of our ancestors took her at her word.

My grandmother grew up outside of Montreal, where her mother died in childbirth, and her father was too poor to care for his four young children. She lived in an orphanage for several years before her father was able to bring her and her brothers back home. At the turn of the century, there were no border walls to keep people out, so people often worked in the U.S. and lived across the border in Canada. The only issue for my grandmother was that she spoke Québécoise, and even back then, Americans didn't like people who didn't speak English.

When she was 18, my grandmother moved to Whitehall, NY, and found work in the silk mill. Like today, people came to the U.S.

looking for work and a better life, which helped create the promise that America is a land of plenty and a path to a decent life. Think Ellis Island. She met my grandfather, a second-generation Irishman, who was brought up on a barge on the Erie Canal. He often spoke of having to retrieve one of his little brothers from the water with a big hook after he'd fallen overboard. Basically, both of my grandparents lived on the promise of a better life and found one, even though they lived through the Depression, two World Wars, and raising eight children in poverty. They survived to meet all 25 of their grandchildren, most of whom graduated from college and fully embraced what this country has to offer its citizens. Unfortunately, I never did learn to speak French, but I inherited a flair for making crepes and a thirst for homemade lemon pie with a three-inch high meringue.

Some professions require you to an oath that serves as a pledge for the way you do your job. For instance, as a lawyer, you have to promise to uphold the rule of law. For doctors, we ask that they take the Hippocrates Oath and do no harm. Soldiers swear to uphold the Constitution, obey their officers and the President. Therapists promise to keep confidential what you talk about in your sessions. And Senators and House of Representatives swear to support and defend the Constitution. There's a whole lot of promising going on, and some are even living up to their promises. Any way we look at it, when a professional takes an oath, it's public and documented. There are regulatory bodies that govern whether or not individuals are adhering to their oaths of office, and if not, they usually end up in a court of law.

Promises that seem to have gone by the wayside are the promises between employees and employers. We no longer make promises to stay for our entire career, nor does an employer promise us that we'll have a job tomorrow, let alone in 20 years. In place of any promises, we've landed in a transactional world where we stay together while we still need each other. The wave of junk bonds financing lever-aged buyouts in the 1980s started a dramatic shift in how we think about corporate structures and employee value. This resulted in cre-ating disposable line items in the company budget, and you and your colleagues are on one of the lines. We're now called human capital. This term helps management objectify the people that are working for them. We're now something like a widget or machine that needs periodic maintenance and will be run hard until the end of its life. I know this sounds cynical, but it's much easier to lay people off and cut salaries when you're not thinking about how Bob Cratchit's son, Tiny Tim, might need an operation. As public companies became slaves to shareholder value, employee value decreased. We're just one item on a profit/loss statement.

I hate to break it to you but if you're looking for a promise of big pay raises, long-term employment and loyalty, you need to think of a business idea you can implement today—well, maybe not today, but after the pandemic dies down. The other option is to keep your resume updated at all times and make friends with as many recruiters in your field as possible. They've become the new guardian angels of the modern era that you call upon when you need a new job.

Although the way we interact in society is constantly evolving, I for one hope we still have as Robert Frost says, "promises to keep." I think our relationships are better when our word is worth something, and our promises to one another create a special bond, a meaningful trust pact. Trust conjures up images of loyalty and fidelity and is the underlying reason we love – it offers safety, protection, and feels di-vine. I promise to keep my promises and will definitely make more. Will you?

....

TWELVE

MY SANDBOX AND YOURS

MUCH OF HUMAN DEVELOPMENT IS SPENT FIGURING OUT WHAT IS mine, what is yours, and what is ours. We've all belted out the refrain, "These are my feelings, damn it." While also remarking, "That's your issue." We only think of the "our" when it's beneficial to both parties such as in, "This is our house and our yard." Living in the U.S. brings out the "mine versus yours" attitude more than in European cultures that have built cooperative, supportive communities. I can't even imagine how wonderful it would have been to have had a one-year leave policy like they have in France for pregnant women. They pay heavier taxes than we do for this benefit, but it would feel worth it as a young mother. As Americans, we don't like being told what to do, nor do many of us like paying taxes.

As a country, we build communities mainly at the local level. Although, we've united to build roads, railways, airports, and military facilities for the betterment and security of all of us. Many of these projects have been executed by private enterprises using taxpayer dollars. It's an example of mine, yours and ours working in unison. One area where we've gone awry is allowing companies to pollute indiscriminately and foul our air and water so that our universal sandbox of wellbeing is at risk. It's a conundrum how to manage all the sandboxes into a collective society that doesn't have winners at the expense of so many losers.

Much of our country's infrastructure was borne out of a combination of creative spirit and opportunistic thirst for power and financial success. The robber barons of the late 1800s and early 1900s were not good sandbox playmates. They were rough and tumble individualists who history has pegged as ruthless industrialists. Their stock-in-trade was making money by building new industries, which is not an undertaking for the faint of heart, think Amazon, Apple, Microsoft, Google, and Facebook. Most notable among these earlier captains of industry were Henry Ford, Cornelius Vanderbilt, Andrew Carnegie, and John D. Rockefeller. Their ventures created jobs for thousands of people while introducing new technologies in car manufacturing, oil refineries, steel, railroads, and shipping. They also enjoyed the luxury of not having to pay personal income tax or a minimum wage to their workers.

Today, we know the names of these early titans primarily because of their large foundations. Luckily for us, the money they made in business greatly contributed to improving all of our lives in areas such as education, medicine, the arts, and civil rights among a few areas of notable causes. Philanthropists built our universities, and hospitals, and public libraries. Today, large foundations like the Gates Foundation are helping to solve world health issues such as eradicating malaria. Over the years, many wealthy Americans have expanded their sandbox and used their millions to help the rest of America. It doesn't matter why they did it -- notoriety, goodwill, or boredom – just that the proverbial "we" benefitted greatly from their generosity.

As individuals, we have to ask ourselves the question: "If I'm the only one thriving, what is my quality of life really?" In essence, if each of us is concerned only about our own sandbox and no one else's, then who can we play with? This is the toddler's dilemma. Our world becomes very small and disconnected when we care only about our own welfare. For those of us who have spent months alone in quarantine, this sounds both boring and very limiting. It also brings back memories of our neighborhood sandlot where there was always a bully throwing sand at the rest of us so we would leave.

In recent years, we've seen a growth in activism by young people, similar to what we experienced in the 1960s when the Vietnam War was raging. More and more young people are getting involved in issues that affect all of us. They are putting their heart and souls and often, their lives, on the line to ensure that the greater good is considered and supported. Climate change is not an individual issue, nor is racial injustice, or income inequality. These types of issues affect all of us in one way or another.

Belonging to a community that nourishes your soul and makes you feel safe and included is very special. I was lucky to grow up in one and then found another in a neighborhood in Chicago where we raised our children. From the day we moved to Lakewood Ave., I felt joy and connection. There was a block party in full gear and about 40 children running down the closed-off street spraying each other with water guns. Parents were chatting with one another and a communal table was laid out for brunch. Everyone took turns welcoming us and offering to help if we needed anything. It was like a scene out of Mayberry in *The Andy Griffith Show*, only urban. For the next 25 years, our family practiced living in a communal sandbox, celebrating holidays with neighbors and friends, mourning 9/11 on each other's porches, raising our children together, and even helping to mop up a neighbor's house after an attic fire. Our sandbox was large and inviting.

One of the biggest eye-openers to how big a sandbox you're in takes place when you travel, especially overseas. You're meeting people casually who either hear your American accent and write you off immediately or think of you as an ally and want to get to know you. For all of us, there's usually judgment associated with opening your sandbox to include strangers. You either feel inclined to connect or reject the "other" as unknowable and fearsome.

When we decided to adopt our son from Vietnam, we didn't think about the fact that we would become a multi-racial family, and what the implications of that would be for all of us. We wanted another child and went for it. We traveled to Ho Chi Minh City to meet our 11-month-old son, not knowing much about his homeland other than that we were at war with it for the better part of 19 years.

Everything about our introduction to Matthew was foreign – the jungle he lived in, the language his nurses spoke to him, how he was fed on the floor, and the fact that no one used a stroller or car seat. It was also monsoon season. I had thought the Midwest was humid in the summer, but soon found out what humidity in the tropics feels like. Dripping with sweat, I carried my new son around the city in a hot, front baby pack, trying to connect with this little, scared human being who was going to be with us forever.

The concept of "yours, mine and ours" takes on new life when you're introducing an adopted baby into your extended family and neighborhood. You're asking for inclusion, and thankfully, our entire family immediately fell in love with Matthew. But, so did our neighbors. They threw a huge party for his one-year-old birthday and helped celebrate his arrival with a great deal of fanfare. It felt wonderful to be part of such an open, caring community of people because we needed them as we swam in unexplored waters.

We learned quickly that not everyone embraced our new family, and some strangers even made disparaging remarks as I pushed him in his new stroller. It hurt, but I wasn't about to let people stuck in the "mine only" way of thinking undermine our family's joy. Throughout the years, Matthew has had to grapple with being the only Asian in our family, and the fact that he doesn't look like any of us. He's also recently had to deal with racism. As Caucasian parents, we have no idea what it's like to have racial slurs thrown at you because of how you look or the color of your skin. Over the past several years, we've learned a lot about the role of community, and how important it is to build a large enough sandbox that everyone can get in.

So, why do some of us like keeping our sandboxes to ourselves? Most of us are not bad and unempathetic people. We don't walk around wishing ill of other people. We can, however, get so engrossed in our own lives that we forget to pick up our heads and ask if anyone needs anything. I know you're thinking, please, don't add anything to my "to do" list.

Human nature comprises both light and dark. We can all be raving lunatics under stress and the kindest, most gentle soul when our bellies are full, and our mortgage is paid. Living in a world as conflicted as ours is now is exhausting. It's hard to focus on my sandbox when our sandbox is on fire. I'm trying to see into your sandbox, but sometimes I can hear you, and other times I can't. We've walked this path before, possibly for thousands of years, which means there's a lot of unpacking to do. It's becoming increasingly clear, however, that because we're linked in a global world, it's time to open our sandboxes to make room for as many people as possible.

Keeping an open heart is the best way I know to create a nourishing and mutually beneficial community. When we enter a conversation already prejudging the content, we've cut off an opportunity to connect. We also can keep ourselves isolated and alone because we're

95

too afraid to accept new people and experiences into our lives. Imagine in your mind's eye what a perfect community for you looks like and who is in it. When you close your eyes and picture this image, do you feel loved and loving?

Section III
I Found Me

Internal peace reigns when we recognize the person inside of us and trust she has our best interest at heart. Embrace her and celebrate her life. She'll always show you the way to meaning and purpose in this lifetime.

THIRTEEN

WHO AM I?

IT'S PRETTY OBVIOUS TO MY FAMILY AND FRIENDS THAT OVER the years, I've devolved into #crankyoldwoman at times. All it took was decades of public transportation and working in downtown, high-rise office buildings to earn that moniker. The culmination of my newfound me happened a few years ago when I found myself standing in the middle of an open office of cubicles and thought to myself, "I'm way too old to do this anymore." Actually, that sentiment was the result of me blowing a gasket after having to swaddle a toxic colleague one more time. It was nothing to be proud of. The worst part was that I had spent a year trying to console other team members who had had similar encounters with this man. I didn't think he would get to me, but then again, I didn't believe my son would send me off the cliff's edge after I was called by the school principal to come get him, yet again! Upon arriving home, Matthew ended up in a face-first, full-body dip in a snowbank – one of my lowest parenting moments, especially because my husband saw the whole thing.

Occasionally, I have had to address myself with the question: "Who am I?" We think we know who we are, and then something scratches an itch, and overboard we go. I confess I am an emotional person in case you haven't picked up on that. But I also know that creating the person I want to be has felt like an endless pottery class where you throw clay pots, and sometimes they stand up on the wheel, and other times they collapse. I've had moments when I looked in the mirror, and the person staring back at me was a complete stranger. And not someone I wanted to know. There have been other times when I've been amused by who I've become. And then there were those times when I couldn't help but recognize that I was a work in progress.

Asking yourself who you really are, sounds like a question posed by a tripping LSD college student in the 1960's. My father, a member of the Greatest Generation, wouldn't abide by that type of question. First of all, it requires introspection and seriously charged psychedelics. Second, it didn't matter who he was in his own mind. He had been faithfully supercharged to be the everyman – living a mainstream life according to the rules of his church, community, parents, and teachers. He was their man.

Granted, people who aren't pondering who they really are may color outside the lines a little, but mostly they prefer to stay within the confines of the generation's mores. If you decide that you'd rather design an out-of-the-box persona, and color way outside the lines, then some options may include weirdo, criminal, hermit, or neighborhood curmudgeon. Any of those options don't make you a party favorite at your family reunion. A friend of mine talks about the time he ran into his cousin at a family picnic and commented on how sunburned his cousin was, thinking he had just returned from a Caribbean vacation. Turns out, his meth lab had exploded, and he had fried his skin. It wasn't a long conversation between the two of them because, frankly, it was hard to see where to take it.

I wasn't always cranky, but living within prescribed notions of correctness has worn me down. However, I'm never worn down for long. After taking the time to sit with my crankiness, I've gone from exhausted to highly energized. I've found a new me that is ready to preach the narrative of breaking out of boxes. I'm now a full-blown activist in the pursuit of freedom -- shedding the "shoulds" and celebrating the whole of me. Understandably, freedom means different things to different people. For some, it means the ability to let your heart sing and your soul fly.

One of the reasons people even have to ask, "Who am I?" is because of the prescription set down for us by others. They pretty much dictate how we'll be seen in the world -- so and so's daughter, honor-roll student, athlete, good kid, and so on. It's, oftentimes, a lack of self-awareness that keeps us from carving out the real you. I remember being puzzled in adolescence about how my insides and outer self didn't seem to match. Now, most teens can say the same thing, so I'm not proffering that I'm unusual. But here I was, a student of literature from a young age who was stealing away as many minutes in a day that she could find to read the classics and cheerleading at football games on the weekend. This moody, pondering young women didn't mesh with the bubbly, cheering girl doing splits across the field. Which one was I really? I suppose I was both.

Humans are multi-faceted beings. Our personas are crafted from the different personality traits we bring forth, creating a fun-house mirror of images of who we are. Let's be honest: most people aren't cranky all the time, nor are we bubbly and chatty all the time, unless you're Lisa from my college English class. The facets of ourselves that we show the world, however, may or may not be who we really are. For example, one of the most moving announcements I ever heard was from a college football player who publicly announced he was gay as the NFL draft was beginning. This took extraordinary bravery to go against the image people had of him and tell the world the truth. He didn't know if he would be accepted or rejected for stating, "This is who I really am." Every person who goes against norms is at risk of being rejected for being different than how people see you and want you to be.

Appearances can be just that – show. You can appear to be confident, but in reality, be very insecure about yourself. You can seem to have the world by its tail and inside be screaming to be let free. We take on appearances because we're expected to be a certain way, and we're trying to fit the mold. Also, we're terrified to confess that we're really something else.

Most of us want luxury trappings because we interpret them as a sign of a successful life. But what if we really preferred a career in non-profit that paid less. Would we be concerned that we would appear less successful? If we never wanted a leadership position in a company would we worry that others would see us as lacking expertise? And if we never married, what would that say about our lovability? In other words, sometimes there's a difference between how you show up in the world and who you really want to be in the world.

One of the hardest parts of trying to fit into a culture is when the culture is so far from who you are. I'm an introvert and have never been comfortable walking into a large conference room where I don't know anyone. I feel awkward and out of place trying to strike up a conversation. Who do you walk up to? What is an opening line? I'm breaking out in a sweat just thinking about it. My sister tells me that neurotic people are some of the most interesting people. Whew. For other people who are extroverts, this is the most natural and exciting place to be. It's who they are!

The best part about giving yourself time and space to figure out who you are at this moment is that when you know who you are, you can behave better. It took me years to realize that I have a blind spot about authority figures. It's definitely an observable characteristic since I'm usually running away from authority. For a long time, I didn't know why I was afraid of it and, therefore, how to behave when I was around it. I learned that I don't have to hate it, and I don't have to fight with it. I also don't have to always flee it. I now understand that I don't trust authority figures because I subconsciously don't think they're benign. There, I said it out loud. And I just admitted that that is part of who I am.

We all have things we like about ourselves, and there are always things we don't like about ourselves. We often focus too much on the negative and not enough on nurturing the positive. I'm not talking about makeup changes here either. I'm talking about the things that make up who you are, such as the way you treat other people, the way you listen or don't, the way you approach a problem and solution, or the way you perceive the world around you. Are you an optimist? Are you confrontational? Are you submissive and insecure? Who are you?

For a few decades now, Professor Brené Brown has brought her research around vulnerability and courage to the public stage. She has helped to bring about a cultural conversation about how claiming our vulnerability is paramount to addressing it.

For every one of us, we find discomfort in the unknown, the imagined, and the new. Our brains go to work overtime when confronted with these types of fears. But they serve as a basis for who we are in the moment. We can change, however, and often do, when it means life will be better and easier. One of the more powerful examples come from people with addictions who take charge of their lives and change.

I do believe people fundamentally know who they are, without having taken the never-ending quizzes on Facebook. You pretty much know if you're part of the 160 IQ genius club or not. You also have a good idea of how athletically gifted you are and whether math and science float your boat or social sciences and literature. What might not be as apparent is the feeling part of who you are, which is both nature and nurture.

There are many examples of nature versus nurture being the underlying reason for your reactions to life. Here are a few nature examples: being a Type A perfectionist that stresses over details or exhibits a high sensitivity to noise that makes you irritable because it hurts your ears. Or even being born with low levels of serotonin that cause episodes of depression. Nurture is far trickier to sort out because it's the result of observations and experiences that cement your emotional reaction to things. For instance, violence does beget violence, hating another for their skin color is taught while kindness and empathy are ingrained from how your family lived their lives. One of the things that always stuck with me is how thoughtful my mother could be. She grew up poor so was always willing to help people in need. She had experienced what it was like to have only one dress and no presents on birthdays. She taught us empathy.

Making changes to the way you show up can be prompted because you want to fit in better or because you want to bring your authentic self to the table. I'm hesitant to use the word "authentic" because it's so overused in today's vernacular, but the sentiment behind it speaks volumes to where society is evolving. The very idea that this is a new phenomenon says to me that we're beginning to strip away the desires of the past and trying to find the essence in our purpose as human beings in today's world. For centuries, our desires centered around survival and acquisition. First, we strategized and hunted to keep ourselves alive. Then we moved to fighting, looting, and controlling to get what we wanted. It's as if we've now arrived at a place where we're asking, "Wait a minute, is this really what life is about?" The idea that I should spend most of my time and effort working to buy things just isn't as satisfying as I thought it was going to be. However, we have to remember that this is a Western conundrum. Survival is still the agenda for the majority of the planet's global population.

Along with the question, "Who am I?" is the question "What does the real me want to do with my life?" It's no accident that we're seeing an uptick in social entrepreneurial ventures, measurement of companies' social impact, and pledges from CEO's to return to community stakeholder value. The truth is that we want to feel good about who we are and what we're doing with our lives. No one really wants to be the jerk in the room or the coward who didn't stand up when they saw something wrong. We want to like ourselves. We desire to be the person who others like as well and feel good when they're around us.

I'm an eternal optimist and believe in the good of humankind. I'm not naïve and do recognize that some people choose the opposite for expediency, power, status, and wealth. However, the majority of people you meet in life are the ones who volunteer their time to hand out food to the homeless, care for animals in shelters, and bring too much food to the potluck. The majority of people go out of their way to make a difference in someone else's life, whether it's through a smile, a hug, or a gift.

Now make a checklist of all the wonderful things you've done for other people this month or this year. It's a great way to affirm that you are the person you aspire to be. It's also an important way to share yourself with others by focusing on what another person needs. In other words, get out of your head and into your heart.

FOURTEEN

JOYOUS RETREATS

BEFORE WE KNEW THAT MY SON NEEDED GLASSES, WE WOULD watch him every Saturday standing idly in the outfield missing every ball hit his way. One sunny day as he was staring off into the distance, he started dancing, and then, what looked like from our bleacher seats, full-throated singing. He was halfway through *High School Musical 1* when one of his peers covering second base shouted at him, "What are you doing?" Matthew just shrugged his shoulders and continued with the melody to *I Don't Dance.*

There is nothing more enjoyable than to watch someone expressing happiness and full-on life. I love watching strangers spontaneously break into song or dance while walking along the street – lost in their own feel-good moment. I can't help but laugh along when I observe children giggling their heads off because of something one of them said. It probably had to do with a bathroom joke. The YouTube videos of flash mobs expressing themselves in music and dance are mesmerizing. And the Instagram posts of a child screaming with glee when they get a new puppy makes me cry joyful tears. There's really nothing like being a witness to someone else's joy.

We haven't had much joy in the world lately and I feel it in my bones. The year 2020 will forever be remembered as the year our lives went from a multi-colored movie to a monochromatic still life. For many, we just went dark. The remnants from a global pandemic, economic collapse, and protests against police brutality sent us all into a tailspin of despair, anger, and sadness. As humans, these are not emotions that we can exist in for long without losing even more of ourselves and our world. Mankind doesn't function well under long periods of chronic hyper stress. It eventually erodes our decision-making abilities, physical health, and emotional wellbeing. In order to regain our balance, we must be able to experience feelings of elation, happiness, and relief. Dear God, at least once in a while.

Meditation has become a cultural phenomenon in the West as our lives have become more and more stressful, and our health has declined. It's a tool to calm the busy and, oftentimes, hysterical mind. Drowning out negative thoughts is the first step to unclogging your brain from fear and despair. I try and meditate every morning so that I enter the day with a clear head. I'm also blocking out the news more than I ever have. Calmness is the first frame to opening yourself up to goodness. You have to be able to see it to feel it.

Joyful memories come in small packages and also large swaths of time. When I think about my wedding day, my heart sings. When I think about raising my children, it makes me smile, most of it anyway. Happiness galvanizes you to forge ahead and embrace life, especially after hard, desperate times. I met my husband after his father died and adopted a beautiful baby boy after I was told I couldn't have any more children. It's up to each one of us to look for a path that helps us find our way back to light-filled joy. Our very life depends on it.

Joy takes place deep down in your core where your belly laughs live. Pleasure is something different. Pleasure is a tactile, physical feeling. When you stroke a cat or dog, you can instantly feel your heart rate go down. Joy takes over your whole being. I remember watching a documentary called *Happiness* that showcased how people from different cultures experience joy, and from what. It was evident that their joy wasn't derived from money, circumstances, or health. It showcased that it's there and available to anyone, at any time, even someone who scavenges garbage all day in an Indian cityscape. It's a state of mind. If you're open to it, joy can be found in what you're doing right now -- in your work, the time spent with your family, interactions with good friends, engaging in hobbies you love, being around your pets as well as other innumerable moments that move your heart and soul. I went to the grocery store today, which during a pandemic is considered a major outing. It brought me incredible joy to be out of the house, around people, even if they were 6 feet away. We mumbled at each other through our masks, and it made me very happy.

I find that taking a walk is a window into joy whenever I'm feeling glum. I'm walking along, and all of a sudden, a male Cardinal flies overhead and lands on a tree branch next to the sidewalk. My heart sings. Or the pink and white peonies are in bloom, and they're the size of my fist. I find joy watching a child learn to ride a bike or a puppy try and figure out how to walk on a leash. They're small things, but the power in them is enough to change my mood, lift my spirits, and make me smile.

It's important to get out of your own way. Now, I'll admit that there are times when I want to wallow in self-pity and dislike everything around me. After a *Boston Herald* reporter called me a flack in his newspaper for a whole year, I was more than agreeable to play the victim. In fact, I was really hacked off when the mayor's office called and said they couldn't take the "flack" anymore, and I would need to leave my post. Humiliation is a recipe for downtrodden emotions, and I wasn't even bothering with the sunny disposition self-talks. I'm pretty sure, if I remember correctly, I just went home got under the bed covers, and stayed there for some time.

After I emerged from my bedsheets, I decided it was time to make a plan. I went to the bookstore, bought a study guide for the GREs, and applied to graduate school. The day I was accepted was definitely a day of heartfelt joy. I moved out of my mourning period and into a new mindset where possibilities existed yet again. Isn't life wonderful, I thought to myself. Sarcasm is one of my specialties as is irony.

When we review the trajectory of our lives it looks more like an EKG reading than a flight log. Circumstances take our lives through inversions, accelerations, and off-road treks. Part of self-reflection is ascertaining whether you can find joy along the way or if you're going to huff and puff every time you trip. We've all met both kinds of people, but the most admirable are those people who still have twinkling eyes and smile lines after experiencing life's hiccups. Why? Because we want to be them. No one really wants to exist in pain and depression. Those emotions are enervating and exceedingly unhelpful when it comes time to move forward and engage with life. It's also hard to establish and maintain relationships with people when you're always crying about how bad your life is. I say this not to minimize legitimate complaints people have whose lives aren't working for them, but rather to set down a perspective about how you show up in the world.

How much control do we really have over our lives? Like in the *Happiness* documentary, joy isn't dependent on your winning the lottery or living in a luxury villa somewhere. Feeling good and being positive is within your control as is how much joy you let in. This is different than trying to control people and events, which, unfortunately, you can't. Well, we all take a good run at controlling other people within our spheres, but it rarely works out well for those involved. I've tried taking charge of my husband's wardrobe for years, and just yesterday, he arrived home from a bike ride in an orange polo shirt and red hiking shorts. No matter how much I try and control the input, the output is never in sync with my desires. What I do have control over are my feelings about his wardrobe selections.

It's definitely within your power to choose to find joy in your life, or not. I don't know if you've ever noticed, but when centenarians are interviewed on television, they always attribute their long lives to either having a positive attitude or never marrying if it's a woman being interviewed. They rarely lived hermetic lives and most never gave up sugar. Also, how they handled stress seems to be a big factor in how they've stayed around so long. They've been enjoying themselves.

Not taking life so seriously, and enjoying it more, could be an antidote to overthinking and overdoing everything. I'm constantly wiping down counters, organizing shelves, and de-cluttering our living spaces. It stresses me out to see crumbs on the countertop. The rest of my family thinks I'm being ridiculous and doesn't care one iota about any of it. The opposite would be to live in utter chaos, which they also wouldn't be up for either. It used to really upset me that my family wasn't as obsessed about clean counters as I was. And then, one day, I caught my nieces laughing about it, and in an instant, I got the message that my obsession was not normal. I'm not sure why it isn't, but it finally dawned on me that I could be stressing about something that wasn't really that important to most people. One more step toward self-actualization!

I really don't like to contemplate the number of things over the years that I have stressed about: lost soccer shoes, being late to a parent's meeting, missing a flight, clean closets, weeding, imperfect hair and makeup, and on and on. There aren't a whole lot of these items that add up to warranting the oncoming heart palpitations or a bit-ing word to another person because I was stressed out. Pretty sure I missed some joyous moments while I was fretting about a chipped nail or a coffee spill. What a waste!

Obviously, there are undeniable stress moments that call for crisis management, but in reality, they're not that common unless you're a transplant surgeon or a mother of more than two children. We heap the stress on and then get depressed that our stress management skills are below average. We work out like maniacs, so the stress doesn't show up around our abdomens, and then try and bluff our way through the day as the cool-cucumber, high-achieving working mother. In retrospect, it's doubtful I ever fooled anyone, certainly not at home.

Part of self-care is taking stock of how you're doing. Are you having a good day? Are you happy? Do you feel fulfilled? This shouldn't be done after an important Zoom client call when your kid was screaming from their nap room that they had to go potty. A good time for self-reflection is during downtime on a walk or run, in the shower, sipping a glass of wine as you stare mindlessly off in the distance, or in the dark as you're waiting alone in the car for your child's gymnastics class to be over. What brought you joy today? What are you smiling about right now? It's important to pay attention.

FIFTEEN

LIVING WITH ME

DATING MY HUSBAND WAS LIKE GOING OUT WITH SIX DIFFERENT guys. I don't mean to imply that he suffers from mental health issues, but early in our relationship, I noticed that he had very distinct personas that expressed different areas of his life. At times, he was a master fly fisherman who tied his own flies and expertly stood in streams for hours on end, casting his line in search of a trout he would catch and release. At other times, he presented himself as a well-read, intellectual college professor whose books I never asked to borrow and who, often, spoke about things I didn't understand. He also was a timid, young man who was terrified of women after a series of missteps. I could go on. In reality, all these personas made up the man I fell in love with and married, and who I would learn to live with. He had already learned to live with all of them.

We each have numerous personas we've tried on over the years. I particularly like my feminist, activist persona while being deeply disturbed by my younger angry, woman thing. I like my caring mommy persona, and dislike my stressed out, working mother persona. I can live with the humorous spouse side of me, but probably should let go of my bitter, righteous wife persona. Figuring out which personas need to stay in the pile is like a game of Poker where you're desperately trying for the Royal Flush -- specific cards all from the same suit that award you the winning hand.

Learning to live with yourself is way different from other people learning to live with you. When I first entered the business world, I was a nice girl who was shy and restrained and very unsure of myself. I was highly competent, but my lack of confidence made me appear more timid than I really was. I found it hard to be around myself. I didn't want to be a person that other people either walked over or ignored. Two things were getting in my way: First, I hated conflict. And second, I hated conflict. What this meant was that whenever anyone questioned my work, opinion, or judgment, I shrunk. It was uncomfortable to live like that.

I countered this persona with becoming a no-nonsense badass that the staff was afraid of. Yikes, girlfriend, could you find some balance? I actually didn't realize that people were afraid to come speak with me until a friend at the company told me. I was horrified! Didn't like this me and, certainly, didn't want to live with her. She was controlling, dismissive, and anxiety-ridden. You can probably picture her since this trajectory is not uncommon in the workplace.

When I lived in Boston, I worked for a woman who got rave reviews from her previous staff as being supportive, a good listener, smart, and so on. I couldn't wait to work for such a great leader. After I went to work for her, I realized that something was amiss. Either her old company had wanted to get rid of her and, therefore, lied about her demeanor or this new position took her out of her body and created a new, unrecognizable persona. She would berate everyone on her executive team and basically tell all of us that she was smarter and more competent than all of us combined. One person artfully remarked that her mother had done a remarkable job raising her to have very high self-esteem. In the end, she was a person I didn't want to live with, not that that mattered to her in the least.

There have been many personas I've discarded along the way because they were no longer useful, or I didn't want to be associated with them anymore. In my junior year in college, I panicked about being an English major with no job skills and decided to get a teaching certificate in the off chance I couldn't get a job in publishing.

This meant I had to student teach at the local high school, which was an old, inner-city school where the first memo I had to read to the students was about entering the building through the doors and not the windows. My mentor was a middle-aged man who walked the classroom aisles with a cane -- not because he had trouble walking but because he felt it gave him authority and magnitude. After I was asked out to the prom by a 10th grader, he thought I could use some shoring up and handed me the cane. I looked like I was carrying a dowsing rod and felt totally ridiculous. There was just no way I was able to take my under-weight, 5 ft. 3 in. self and project physical superiority. I quickly handed the cane back to the teacher and continued to find a persona that was better suited to my physique and age. It turned out that empathetic champion was a better fit, and one I could live with.

Personas start young and become part of a yarn ball that you have to unravel when you're ready to knit that cardigan you've been eying. The material, the assembly and the end product all go into developing the person you are most able to live with. I started out being told I was "cute" on the one hand and on the other being chastised as an "ingrate" by my father when I didn't do what I was told. Thereby, I learned that my cuteness wasn't a deciding factor if I ticked off my dad. I was athletic while having no aptitude whatsoever with anything to do with arts and crafts. My sister and mother used to lock me in the sewing room when it was time to make my prom dress. They weren't interested in participating in my fits as I repeatedly ripped out the seams to a dress that never fit right. It was maddening for them and me. To this day, whenever I drive by a Joann's fabric store, I have a traumatic flashback. What was evident from this task was that I didn't have the interest or temperament for crafts but could endlessly persevere through pain and disappointment at ski trials, trying again and again to improve my slalom time.

There are just so many sides to who we are. There have been times when I've been self-satisfied with who I had become, and then again, there have been moments when I got a quick look at a certain aspect of my persona and felt disappointed. Self-hating is not something you should do for long periods since it's highly unproductive and a waste of time or energy. I suppose I've felt most satisfied when I've worn my artistic, empowered, and loving self in public and private. I've enjoyed going home with her the most. She's the one that I feel most sure about, but I definitely have more than three personas to draw from.

What I've found is that you don't have to be a famous artist or writer to embody the persona of one. Writers are storytellers who relish character details and storyline throughputs. They imagine worlds unseen and create intricate situations for characters that are complex and sometimes messy, just like life. They draw from what they know and then embellish. They make us feel something. I've spent hours getting lost in the worlds of Isabel Allende, Tony Morrison, Louise Erdrich, Jhumpa Lahiri, and Amy Tan. These modern-day writers opened up unknown worlds to me and left me wanting more.

Owning an empowered persona can be a two-sided sword. On the one hand, you're assured and fiercely dedicated to what you believe, and then again, you can be off-putting and tough to reckon with. My heroes are women who are empowered to change worlds, apologize when necessary, and listen with both their heart and soul. I think Oprah Winfrey is a good example of these traits. She obviously has a big heart, isn't afraid to speak her mind, and has changed the world for the better. She's a seeker, which I also admire since it doesn't appear anyone ever learns it all in one lifetime.

Being a person who creates light-filled experiences for other people and works in service to what others need is a moral tradition I learned at church. Although I no longer consider myself a Catholic, I haven't relinquished all the teachings I learned as a child. For decades, Mother Theresa symbolized to the world a loving spirit dedicated to helping others. She was an extreme example of a generous and caring person. I've tried to bring that spirit to all my relationships. Giving another person solace, hope, and love is part of a persona that I strive to inhabit.

When you're training children to be social creatures, it's difficult to always lead them in a loving, moderated way so that they develop personas that are positive and helpful in their lives. A friend's mother once told me that she always made sure to never spank her children in anger. I'm not sure if she never spanked her kids then, because when else would you swat the backside of a child? What I do know is that the way in which you model behavior influences what personas your child chooses. I'm not going to own all their behavior, or choices, and ways of being in the world, but I do know that our children are kind, caring people because of how we taught them to relate to others. They are also masterful at working over their parents.

Whenever my daughter wanted to influence a decision, she would put together a PowerPoint or write a white paper to explain her choices and then end with an ask. Her most strategic presentation came when she was in high school and wanted to pierce her eyebrow. She had already done it and just wanted us not to ground her. I think she also wanted us to understand why it was so important to her. She had learned that my first instinct is to say "no" and that her father would endlessly try and talk it through with her. She avoided both reactions by coming to us prepared while also anticipating our questions. Today as a professional, she uses the same cool-headed persona that critically analyzes a problem, reasons it out, and then articulates it in writing. I'm so glad we could help.

Being able to live with yourself is critical to your happiness. People who struggle with liking themselves have a harder time seeing themselves in the world any other way than as a victim or a perpetrator. Either option turns you into a grumbling, old loner. One of the most well-known is the character Ebenezer Scrooge from *A Christmas Carol* and look what happened to him – three terrifying nights of reckoning. Granted, the entertainment industry has made boatloads of money telling the story of the victim and perpetrator, but who wants to have to go through that much transformation to find peace. It's so much better to witness it on screen than in your own life.

How you show up in the world is the result of reactions to experiences, heroes you admire, and your own emotional makeup. You wear your personas like a fitted glove if they're right for you and baggy jeans if they're just not working out. I recommend going through your closet and keeping the ones that make you smile and fill you with pride and tossing the others in a trash bag. Be someone you want to go home with at night. It's worth the time and effort it takes to coordinate the best ensemble.

SIXTEEN

GRATITUDE

THERE'S MUCH TO BE GRATEFUL FOR WHEN YOU DECIDE TO appreciate the spoils of life. I'm even grateful that I come from a large, wacky, dysfunctional family that includes three siblings, 41 cousins, and 20 aunts and uncles, representing just about every walk of life and political stripe. Several of my cousins I've never met, but I'm pretty sure with our strong DNA I'd recognize them if we were to meet on the street. I'm also grateful my husband is an only child, has only three cousins, and grew up with parents who were adults and relatively free of mental health issues. My family has most of the diagnoses covered.

Gratitude is one of those things that happens when you bother to look around you. It's a comparative measure of how great your life is and how much you appreciate what it has offered you. It takes years to appreciate your mishaps, but if you're living in the positive zone, you come to grab the lessons they offered and run with them. Some of my moments of heartache, taught me lessons that left me better able to handle the world than before: learning to love unconditionally, living in humility, forgiveness, being flexible and agile, and letting go, to name a few.

The greatest gift of my life has been the relationships I've forged over the years. We're not meant to live alone on an island and, therefore, require deep, meaningful ties to nurture us along the way. What would my sister have done if I hadn't been there when she mistakenly colored her hair green, and I laughed so hard I cried? And what would my childhood have been like without close friends, Betsy and Greta, who taught me that threesomes are sometimes thorny to manage, but good friends work it out? And, more than anything, what would my life have been like if I hadn't met Phyllis 30 years ago? Phyllis was my mother-in-law and the most wonderful woman I have ever known.

I was first introduced to Phyllis the Christmas before my husband and I were married. She had moved to Boulder, CO, to retire and spent all of her time volunteering for the Boulder County AIDS Project. The first thing I remember thinking on Christmas morning was how great it must have been to be an only child, and next, what a lovely woman my husband had as a mother. Over the years, Phyllis taught me many things, but the greatest gift was how to love unconditionally. I felt so loved by her – secure, supported, and listened to. She was always present with whomever she sat across from, making them feel important and infinitely interesting. She smiled easily and jumped in to help before she was even asked. People were drawn to her, especially children, in a way I hadn't seen before. She didn't judge, and I rarely ever heard her say a negative word about anyone, even if they deserved it, including her ex-husband.

People come and go in our lives, but the times we spend together are crucial to our development and theirs. I'm fortunate to have made good friends over the years that have given me sustenance when I needed it most. They weren't just there during the big things, however, such as the birth of my daughter or my son's adoption. They were there to drink wine with and talk about our jobs, marriages, and travel plans. They knew the details of my life, and I knew theirs. Human connection is the thing I crave the most and to which I place the highest honor.

Although I'm very grateful for our family's good health, experiences and opportunities, I know that life wouldn't be as ripe and full without the people who have come into it and made it tastier and bigger. If I had never met my dear Jamaican friend Anna Kay while living in New York, I would never have had a chance to hear the lilt in her voice as she described paragliding and falling into a farmer's muddy pigsty. I can't imagine what college would have been like without Georgina and her Nogales, AZ, family who introduced me to Mexican food and the jail where Poncho Villa was imprisoned. My life would have been so much smaller if I hadn't shared apartments, children, and block parties with Lois, Laurie, Mar'Sue, Lynn, Gael, Tracy, Anne, and Sonia.

Life is filled with so many wonderful moments that need to be celebrated and acknowledged. We were lucky to live in a neighborhood where people loved to celebrate. There was never any shortage of front porch get-togethers or absurdly extravagant block parties. I am grateful that I got to know all the children on our block and be there while they grew into beautiful human beings. There's nothing like having a front-row seat to a child's first day at kindergarten or when they finally take the training wheels off and ride on two wheels – party time!

I appreciate the big things that happened in my life as well -- the beautiful home we built and the gardens we planted. I even smile when I think of all the projects we never got to before we sold it. Big things happen every few years or even every few decades, but they stand out because they can change the course of your life. When you look at the road you've traveled, you can see perfectly the fork that took you down one path instead of another. When I left the Northeast and moved to the Midwest, I never dreamed what this city would hold for me. I didn't know that I would find a large, urban landscape that lived more like small towns knitted together than an anonymous metropolis filled with skyscrapers. I didn't know that I would spend so much time on a Great Lake or that I would be at ease smiling and saying hello to complete strangers as I walked the streets of downtown. Who knew?

One of the things I appreciate about our family, well, three out of four of us, is our sense of adventure. We're pretty much game to try most things. We love to travel, learning about the history of a place, and meeting people who open doors to worlds we never imagined. One of the more profound books I've ever read is Dr. Seuss', *Oh, the Places You'll Go.* One quote, in particular, says it all for me, "You're off to Great Places! Today is your day! Your mountain is waiting, So... get on your way!"

I'm so appreciative of the opportunities I've had to travel to exotic places like China and Vietnam. It was there, for the first time, that I began to understand what it feels like to be a minority, not speak a language, and have no earthly bonds to a place. Their language is so different from ours that you can't piece together one word. It's as though you can't find a way in. You're totally dependent on your acting ability to ask a question, which makes for some pretty funny exchanges and some not so funny dinners. These experiences, however, provided me with a window into what it would feel like to be a new immigrant in America – excited but lost as well. I can't imagine the anxiety of knowing that you have to make a living fast to survive in your new country. Most of us have never felt that level of pressure. I'm grateful that my travel experiences have given me compassion and empathy for newcomers.

One of the benefits of finding gratitude is that your outlook on life becomes more positive. You look for the good in others instead of judging people for their shortcomings. Granted, that's a leap for most of us. One way to change your outlook is to spend less time reading and watching the news. Media stories are mostly made up of the car crashes of life, which makes us not like each other very much. In fact, I think that's the point. I've recently struggled with this because I was trained as a journalist and really like news, but I find myself with a stomachache after watching the nightly news programs and over-whelmed with feelings of helplessness. I'm grateful I can turn it off.

Curiosity is a great human quality. Our need to figure things out, solve problems, and learn about things we don't know anything about is one of the most positive things you can do for yourself. Aren't you grateful for our public libraries and free online courses? What a gift! I recently had to learn how to put a website together that included integrating several plugins. I was terrified. Luckily, my brother helped since he is more technologically savvy than I am, but I did it! I actually figured it out. What a great feeling!

There have been many adages spoken about attitude over the years, but for me, Winston Churchill said it best, "Attitude is a little thing that makes a big difference." And, of course, he needed to believe that considering what was on his plate. A positive attitude and deep gratitude are the tools we need to carry with us at all times. They take the sting out of loss and heartache and bring meaning and love into our lives. They shine a light on the world and make you smile at the thought of another day. They are your friends.

If you haven't started one, try keeping a daily gratitude list. It will change your mindset as you start your day. It keeps you present and mindful of where you are today, not yesterday, and not into the future. What are you grateful for today?

....

FINDING MEANING AND PURPOSE

As the Grateful Dead once sang, "What a long, strange trip it's been," but I hope reading about my experiences has been an enjoyable one and has helped motivate you to do your own self-discovery. I promise, it isn't a waste of time to think about your dreams and how you're showing up in the world. Take the time to understand what triggers you and why you react a certain way to situations and experiences, so the next time you can respond with calmness and clarity. Be patient with yourself while also committing to expanding your self-awareness. Digging in to find your true essence will bring about a consciousness that will help you thrive in your daily life. And isn't that really what we all want?

Oftentimes, it's trial and error that unlocks the realization of who we really are and what's important to us. The key to thriving is to keep persevering and not let life's struggles get you down. It's also embracing the understanding that life changes, and you will move on from low points to better days.

As I said before, I'm an eternal optimist. I've also witnessed the ebb and flow of life and can attest to its winding, fluid nature that moves you like a roaring river in spring past despair and onto joy, and then again, to disappointment, and back to contentment. Don't be afraid of the lows of life. They're our teachers and serve as the guides to finding what we really want out of life. We don't need to experience poverty to know that we want to be secure financially, but we do need to understand what we are willing to do to make money and how much we need to be comfortable. The yardstick is different for different people.

The final essays in Section III, "I Found Me," are meant to put you in the driver seat for defining who you are and how you relate to the rest of society. Relationships and community are vital components in one's life. They dictate how well you'll thrive and grow. They also give us an outlet for our gifts and talents and provide us with a path to become part of central casting in this overall enterprise -- life on Earth. In this crazy, ever-evolving human creation, we have a role to play, and it's our job to contribute and not just take.

I look forward to meeting you along life's many paths while we all work to make life better for ourselves and others. Living life to its fullest, and not being afraid to be our best and do our best. Dreaming big and always being curious. Embracing empathy and compassion for others and devoting ourselves to a creative life that offers sunrises and sunsets. After all, this really is your life.

Peace always,

Sarah Wilcox

ABOUT THE AUTHOR

AFTER MANY YEARS OF WORKING IN CORPORATE OFFICES AND START-UP warehouses, Sarah decided to come home to Chicago and offer career and life coaching services to women based on what she knows about putting it all together. This includes what happens when you try and renovate a house, raise a two year old, and study for your MBA degree all at the same time. It also includes how to fail and get up again, and how to celebrate your hard-earned wins.

Sarah started her career as a journalist in New York City, working for the only magazine her father would read, GOLF magazine. In a twist of fate, she then found herself working in marketing for various healthcare companies over the next few decades. She ended her corporate career as an Executive Vice President for a large, well-known advertising agency before entering the entrepreneurial world, which is where it got really interesting.

Throughout Sarah's career, she has been a mentor and counselor to women who were trying to manage home and work life, move up the corporate ladder, and start their own companies. As a business leader, she has always been passionate about influencing corporate cultures to be more inclusive of diversity, and to the unique gifts and talents women bring to the table. She started her career at the fore-front of the Women's Movement and has never wavered from her advocacy of gender pay equality as well as ensuring that corporate policies make it possible for women to excel at work while continuing as the primary caregiver at home.

Sarah has a master's in business from Northwestern University's School of Management and finished the coursework for her master's in fine arts at Emerson College in Writing and Latin American Literature. She received her B.A. from SUNY at Buffalo in Journalism and English Literature. Sarah lives in Chicago with her husband, where they raised their two children.

www.ingramcontent.com/pod-product-compliance
Lightning Source LLC
LaVergne TN
LVHW051417080426
835508LV00022B/3121